RURAL DEVELOPMENT

> *"My path, as you know, lies in the domain of quiet, integral action and thought, my units must be few and small, and I can but face human problems in relation to some basic village of cultural area. . . ."*
>
> — **RABINDRANATH TAGORE**
>
> (From *Essays and Exchanges between Rabindranath Tagore and L.K. Elmhirst,* Visva-Bharati, 1961)

About the Author

Gobinda C. Mandal, *(b. 1916)* obtained M.A., doctorate and Jubilee Research Gold Medal plus Prize from the University of Calcutta. He taught economics in a few colleges under the Calcutta University and also in the Research & Training Section of the Indian Statistical Institute, Calcutta. In 1960 he was appointed Director (Professor) of the Agro-Economic Research Centre, Visva-Bharati, Santiniketan. He was appointed a Specialist of UNESCO to its "Projects of Strengthening Agricultural Training in the Philippines" during 1967-71 and a Visiting Professor in the University of Agriculture, Malaysia during 1976-77. He taught post-graduate courses in economics, conducted numerous research projects, guided Ph. D. scholars as their Supervisor, attended international conferences and is author of a large number of books and articles including 'Technology, Growth and Welfare in Indian Agriculture'. Dr. Mandal is currently associated with Elmhirst Institute of Community Studies at Santiniketan as its Honorary Professor and Consultant.

RURAL DEVELOPMENT
Retrospect and Prospect

GOBINDA C. MANDAL

CONCEPT PUBLISHING COMPANY PVT. LTD.
NEW DELHI-110059

ISBN: 978-81-7022-396-2

First Published 1992

Published and Printed by

Concept
Since 1974

Concept Publishing Company Pvt. Ltd.
A/15-16, Commercial Block, Mohan Garden,
New Delhi-110059 (India)
T: 91-11-41101460
E: publishing@conceptpub.com, *W*: www.conceptpub.com

To
The Memory
of
L.K. ELMHIRST
Who Pioneered
Rural Reconstruction
in Collaboration with
RABINDRANATH TAGORE

PREFACE

THE PRESENT book is a book of ideas and opinions written intermittently over a number of years from 1969. It is based on experience derived from research projects undertaken by me in the Philippines, at the Agro-Economic Research Centre, Visva-Bharati and Elmhirst Institute of Community Studies.

The Projects may be specifically mentioned as "Cooperative Studies" undertaken as a training cum research project incidental to my UNESCO assignment in the Philippines, "Continuous Village Surveys", "Understanding Rural Moneylenders in West Bengal" and "Technology Growth and Welfare in Agriculture – A case study in West bengal" at the Agro-Economic Research Centre, Visva-Bharati and "The Problem of Literacy and Education among Scheduled Caste Girls" which was undertaken at the Elmhirst Institute of Community Studies at Santiniketan. Of course, material picked from survey projects was supplemented by data from secondary sources. It is needless to say that much of the work was done incidentally to the proiects under reference.

The book consists of 10 chapters. The first chapter is an attempt at understanding Indian rural society by making a comparison with Japan. The second chapter is a theoretical thinking on the possibility of village self-sufficiency relating to the pioneering ideas of Mahatma Gandhi and

Rabindranatha Tagore. The third chapter examines how economic growth through trade and rural development can be made compatible with equity. The fourth chapter seeks to ascertain how far study of different types of villages observed at a particular point of time can be used to indicate a process of growth. Land question, the condition of scheduled caste and tribes, rural credit, role of decentralised planning and role of cooperation are subjects for discussions in the subsequent chapters. Chapter 10, the concluding one focuses on the significance of a cultural revolution.

Readers may find that all these are crucial questions of rural development. The emphasis of the study is on decentralised planning because of its root in the tradition of Indian rural society and its concentration on intensive utilization of local resources.

Information and statistical data related to topics of Chapter 2, Chapter 3 and Chapters 7 to 9 are brought up-to-date in Appendices A, B and C respectively. Recent information about specific programmes of rural development connected with Chapter 8 are presented in Appendix D. Appendix E briefly covers some recent discussions on the question of tenancy and land-ownership.

It may be noted that though the study attempts to provide all relevant information about recent developments in our rural economy, its main thrust is on the inner principle rather than on information. Understanding the motivation of rural change both by introspection and retrospection is the central purpose of the study. It is hoped that the study would provide some insight into the problem and process of rural development.

My exchanges with Dr. A.K. Dasgupta, Emeritus Professor, Jawaharlal Nehru University, Dr. S.R.

Sen, a past President of the International Association of Agricultural Economists and Dr. Samar K. Datta provided stimulus to this work. I am grateful to them. Assistance from my past colleagues of the Agro-Economic Research Centre, Visva-Bharati, is thankfully acknowledged.

Santiniketan,
August, 1991

G.C. MANDAL

CONTENTS

LIST OF TABLES

1

COMMUNITY VERSUS MARKET RELATIONS IN THE AGRARIAN ECONOMY

A VILLAGE is a macro-entity in a miniature form comprising a community of people who have certain degree of cohesion among themselves due to living in a small contiguous area.[1] This area is well-defined. Thus, the village is a primary geographical community.

Its cohesion promoted a natural cooperation in the form of exchange of products and services among its members. A basically agricultural community, it could attain in the earlier times self-sufficiency in social and economic spheres of the life which was substantially maintained even in the later period. Villagers could meet most of their vital needs within the frontier of their village so long as life was simple.

At the beginning of the 19th century Dr. Francis Buchanan, a medical officer of the East India Company was commissioned by the Government to conduct an enquiry into the economy of India. From his direct observations the following pattern of distribution of a heap of 2400 seers (about 4800 lbs) of grain among the constituents of a village near Bangalore was documented (Table 1.1).[2]

TABLE 1.1: Constituents of an Early 19th Century Village

Category	Seers
Village Priests	5
Village Charity	5
Village Astrologer	1
Village Brahman	1
Village Barber	2
Village Potter	2
Village Blacksmith	2
Village Washerman	2
Village Measurer	4
Village Beadle	7
Village Chief	8
Village Accountant	10
Village Watchman	10
Village Accountant	45
Village Chief	45
Conductor of Water	20
	169

"Thus a payment of 5.25 per cent of the produce of the fields secured to the villagers the professional services of the barber, the potter and the blacksmith, the priest and the astrologer. Of the remainder, the Deshmukh of Zemindar claimed 10 per cent and the balance was divided equally between the Government and farmer".[3]

The cohesive character of the village naturally enabled it to develop a local self-government by virtue of which it was possible for the village community to survive all sorts of tussles and turmoils that swept over the country from time-to-time.

According to a statement made by Sir Charles

Metcalfe as early as in 1830 the village communities in Northern India were little republics, having nearly everything they wanted within themselves.[4] They seemed to last where nothing had lasted. Dynasty after dynasty tumbled down, revolution succeeded to revolution; Hindu, Pathan, Moghul, Maratha, Sikh, English were masters in turn; but the village communities, each one forming a separate little state in itself continued to be the same and conceivably contributed more than any other cause to the preservation of the people of India through all revolutions and changes which they had suffered and it was in a high degree conducive to their happiness, and to the enjoyment of a great portion of freedom and independence.

It is a matter of great regret that India which had been the "earliest home of village communities" that maintained internal security of the country for thousands of years declined under the excessively centralized administration of foreign rulers from the West.

The ideal of village community was greatly upheld by Mahatma Gandhi and the Poet Rabindranath Tagore as a model of village self-sufficiency and self-reliance. In fact, Tagore wanted to revive the village community as a non-political base for social regeneration in rural India where majority lived. Rural reconstruction was the very basis of his nationalism. Through an appropriate work-oriented education it was directed to develop the creative and cooperative power of the rural man by which the basic needs of life could be satisfied.

In Japan, too, natural village communities, namely 'Shuraku' or 'Buraku' occupy a place of great importance. These are primary units of a territorial community which formed the base of cooperatives for progressive agricultural production.

Most of the 'Shurakus' (90.3%) were established prior to Meiji era.[5] Ishikawa observed that community relations were still functioning in the 'Shuraku'. The 'Shuraku's developed the tradition of villagers' joint operations in the maintenance of ordinary and agricultural roads by contribution of labour or by contributions of money for hiring labour.[6]

There were remarkable changes in the Japanese agricultural society in the post-Second World War period. "One is that despite the tremendous decrease in population engaged in agriculture (i.e. a decrease of 51.5% between 1960 and 1978), the decrease in the number of farm households was much smaller (only 22.5%). As a result the proportion of part-time farm households to total farm households was 87.5 per cent in 1978.

"Among several types of Farm-cooperatives, groups for contract farming using large-scale tractors and other agricultural machines on the basis of the work of operator farmers coming from full-time farm households were predominant.[7]

Within the system of Groups for contract Management the tendency for part-time farm households to desert agricultural production by simply entrusting individual operations to outside operators accelerated. With the increasing sizes of machines and equipment, the size of the group was enlarged far beyond the social range of 'Shuraku', with the result that the community-consciousness of the 'Shuraku' was finally on the wane. This was particularly true with the younger generations.

According to Rabindranath Tagore, Poet and Philosopher, traditional unity amidst apparent heterogeneity has through all ages been an essential characteristic of the Indian rural society. European unity had been rooted in force, but Indian unity had always been fostered by the inner process of harmony.[8] Strife is inherent in the system of political unity of Europe which is always pitted against foreign elements—but not harmoniously self-contained within itself. It is beset by tensions between man and man, between kings and subjects, between the rich and poor. In this system individuals or groups are not held together by a spirit of service to the common — they are engaged in a desperate conflict each preventing other from rising to power. The Indian society as distinguished from the Western is composed of households and village communes centering round which have developed conventions regulating the pattern of social life in India.[9] The traditions of occupation cum caste hierarchy reconciled the conflicts of competition and tempered the rarity of wealth and power. The supremacy of the Brahmins (the priestly caste) was recognized on intellectual grounds and not on the basis of wealth. And this was maintained in harmony with the process of democratization of economic and educational opportunities—the process of the rich sharing their fortunes through various mediums.[10]

> "Creation of community consciousness would in large measures amount to a revival, as in almost all parts of the country we can recall a past in which community of interest and of corporate action was realized. Considerations of individual or sectional project, and of enforcement by coercive action are the very negation of the real merit of community feeling. It is quite possible that some type of community action may entail a power of sanction, including a thing like *Suddhi Prayog*, technique of purification, in which the supporters of the community may impose a

> penance or punishment on themselves to induce a change of heart, and then of action in the dissenter. Several other variants of such techniques which rely on moral, rather than physically coercive sanctions can be easily thought of. In most of these respects we always have some tradition to draw upon. But to ensure progress and development what must be newly emphasized is dynamism of purpose which frankly is alien to our past."[11]

Unfortunately this very dynamism emerging from the pressure of growth of market forces which was due to various factors, such as urban-industrialization, accumulation of finance capital, transportation, expanding exchange relations, technological progress etc. broke down the age-old community relations of Indian rural society that was predominantly marked by patron-client relationship.

The developments that sharpen division of labour between country and town, between production and intercourse which resulted in the widening of trade through specialized merchants weakened the community relations of rural society. A description of this process may be found in the following statement of Marx and Engels:[12]

> "Manufacture and the movement of production in general received an enormous impetus through the extension of intercourse which came with the discovery of America and the sea-route to the East Indies. The new products imported thence, particularly the masses of gold and silver which came into circulation had totally changed the position of the classes towards one another, dealing a hard blow to feudal landed prosperity and to the workers. The expeditions

> of adventurers, colonization and above all the extension of markets into a world market, which had now become possible and was daily becoming more and more a fact, called forth a new phase of historical development."

The period from the middle of the 17th century up to the end of the 18th witnessed expansion of commerce and navigation at a rate higher than manufacture, turning colonies into big consumers.

It is quite natural that the advent of British rule in India bringing in its train its own relationship with the current world forces to bear on the Indian rural economy, too, would thus be substituting market relations for community relations.

At this point, following Ishikawa, a retrospective view of different types of community relations prevailing in Asia is taken.[13] In Japan community relations were inherent in the villages formed by quasi-kinship group where lands were held under the management of hereditary main families rooted in the subordination of branch families and servants who were assured subsistence in return of labour services rendered to the former. The economic status of the branch families and the servants, however, underwent considerable improvement under commercialization of agriculture. The system of direct management of farms by petty landlords played a crucial part in the technological transformation of agriculture in Japan in the Meiji Period (1968-1911) that reinforced the development of market relations. The subsequent period was characterized by the predominance of peasant-owned farms which heightened technological progress in conformity with some remnants of community relations. In precommunist China community relations were implicit in some joint farm-operations of the class constituting a village. In India a village was composed of cultivators, artisans and labourers, status of each category being determined by caste and each assured of a share as has been seen earlier. Production relations in farm-production were those of landlord—client type. However, in India caste-system which once ensured social peace by assigning to each a station in life and assuring subsistence to each degenerated into a stagnating force stripped of egalitarian principle.

Diverse situations caused variation in the application of community principle. In hierarchical society it was used as a tool of assuring minimum subsistence for all. With the growth of fixed capital it became instrumental to fuller utilization of enhanced production capacity. Moreover, exposed by the forces of market economy to the exploitation of urban merchants, the rural society could utilize community principle in the form of cooperatives to safeguard its interests. Community principle could also be utilized as a measure against uncertainty. The cooperative "grain golas" (foodgrains store) of India could be mentioned by way of illustration. In fact the cooperative movement of India grew up mostly as a resistance to the extortions of money-lenders from rural borrowers.

Yujiro Hayami still believes: "Self-sustaining growth of the rural economy in developing countries cannot be expected without a policy that makes positive use of indigenous community relations and local market organizations as a basis of modern rural development institutions."[15]

NOTES

1. G.C. Mandal and Associates, Economics of Rural Change—A study in East India, Firma K.L.

Mukhopadhyay, Calcutta 1974.

2. Ramesh Dutt, *The Economic History of India*, Vol. 1, Government of India, 1960 p. 141.
3. *Ibid*, p. 141.
4. *Ibid*, pp. 267-268.
5. Shigeru Ishika, 'Peasant Families and Agrarian Community in the Process of Economic Development' in Llyod G. Reynolds, ed., *Agriculture in Development Theory*, Yale University Press, New Haven, 1975.
6. *Ibid.*
7. *Ibid.*
8. Rabindranath Tagore, "Bharatbarser Itihas" (A vision of Indian History) in his book *Swadesh.*
9. *Ibid.*
10. *Ibid.*
11. D.G. Carve, "Community and Cooperations" in Gobindachandra Mandal, ed., Seminar on Human Factor in the Growth of Rural Economy Agro-Economic Research Centre, Visva-Bharati, Santiniketan, 1962.
12. Marx and Engels, *The German Ideology*, Progress Publishers, Moscow, 1976, pp. 77-78.
13. Shigeru Ishikawa, "Peasant Families and Agrarian Community in the Process of Economic Development" in Lloyad G. Reynolds, ed., *Agriculture in Development Theory*, Yale University Press, New Haven, 1975.
14. G.C. Mandal, "A View of the Impact of Sriniketan Experiment" in Gobindachandra Mandal, ed., Seminar on Human Factor in the Growth of Rural Economy – *Proceedings* of Rabindranath Tagore Birth Centenary Celebrations, Vol. VII, Agro-Economic Research Centre, Visva-Bharati, Santiniketan, 1962, p. 38.
15. Yujiro Hayemi, "Community, Market and State", Elmhirst Memorial Lecture in *Proceedings* of the Twentieth International Conference of Agricultural Economists, Dartmouth for IAAE, 1989.

2

THE IDEA OF VILLAGE-SELF-SUFFICIENCY

THE IDEA of village-self-sufficiency fits very well into the model of a decentralized economy, the core of Gandhian economic thinking and his plan of new education—*Nai Talim*. Gandhiji's principles of economics are very well-integrated with his philosophy of living. The present chapter does not propose to undertake an exploration in the vocabulary of Gandhian economics but attempts an application of its intrinsic logic to different situations.

Profit Maximization vs Maximum Utilization of Man-power

The central theme of Gandhian economics is maximization of the creative power of man and not profit maximization, since it is an offspring of the struggle to eradicate poverty. Profit maximization leads to the maximization of social welfare and maximum utilization of man power but only as long as profit is unimpared and has not declined. Moreover, there is no guarantee that profit-maximization would always conform to maximum utilization of the human resources. The whole array of Marx-Keynes-Harrod-Domar models of economic development is centred on the basic problem of harmonization of profit and maximum use of the human capacity for production. The Gandhian model emphasizes creativeness rather than acquisition,—self-fulfilment rather than self-aggrandisement. Profit-maximization has an undefined limit, whereas services and creativeness are both philosophically and materially self-contained. In a system where economic reward is just proportional to work and service, pursuit of wealth is harmonized with the principle of self-sufficiency.

Economic significance of national independence was national self-sufficiency. For 250 years India supplied Britain with raw materials which were returned to India as finished goods resulting in recurring net loss of raw materials and perpetual dependence on Britain for some basic needs such as clothing. Thus, the struggle for political independence took the form of a struggle for economic self-sufficiency on a national plane.

The spinning wheel introduced by Gandhiji in the struggle against poverty was extensively used prior to the British period. Such small industries, however, not being adequate for the nationwide demand, failed to compete with the British capitalist industries and declined. Moreover, the Indian textile industries fractionally met the need of the country. The practical Gandhian ideology of national, regional or village-self-sufficiency was the natural outcome of acute poverty resulting from slavish dependence upon a foreign country for the satisfaction of an elemental need. It aimed at preventing wastage of manpower and channelling it into creation of simple goods not towards luxurious abundance but harmonious and peaceable self-satisfaction.

Adam Smith, the founder of classical capitalistic economics, prescribed division of labour or specialization supported by expansion of market as the road to prosperity. His was the doctrine of surplus and restless searching for markets for the disposal of surplus and running from one peak of prosperity to another.

The Gandhian system was not to search for markets but self-satisfaction. Utilization of human capacity for the satisfaction of human needs was the key-not of his philosophy. The economic horizon of Adam Smith was not limited by the bound of human capacity—it was subject to the dynamics of expansion inherent in surplus.

Living Within One's Means

If self-sufficiency is crystallised into a doctrine, it would reveal itself in a number of aspects. Foremost of all, it is the old and wise doctrine of living up to one's means.

The deficit financing in Indian planning is equivalent to making investments which are not adjusted to the savings of the previous period. The obvious consequence is inflation unless spending is instantaneously followed by proportionate rise in production or supply of consumer goods which is far from the reality. Inflation is not only symptomatic of a basic imbalance between savings and investment, but it develops into a desperately competitive bid for maintaining or improving relative position between one section of the community and another. The most important wastage of inflation consists in making profits simply by selling at higher prices and preventing real resources from coming into fuller use for the production of more goods. This is a deep-seated malady ingrained in foreign borrowing as well as deficit financing. Borrowing is simply an attempt to live beyond means.

A few of Gandhiji's own sayings are quoted below to demonstrate the simplicity of the logic of self-sufficiency and his keen perception of reality.[1]

> "When production and consumption both become localized, the temptation to speed up production, indefinitely and at any price, disappears. All the endless difficulties and problems that our present-day economic system presents, too, would then come to an end.
>
> Simple homes from which there is nothing to take away require no policing; the palaces of the rich must have strong guards to protect them against dacoity. So must huge factories. Rurally organized India will run less risk of foreign invasion than urbanized India, well equipped with military, naval and air forces.
>
> My idea of village Swaraj is that it is a complete republic, independent of its neighbours for its vital wants, and yet interdependent for many others in which dependence is a necessity. Thus every village's first concern will be to grow its own food crops and cotton for its own cloth. It should have a reserve for its cattle, recreation and playground for adults and children. Then if there is more land available, it will grow useful money crops, thus excluding *ganja*, tobacco, opium and the like. The village will maintain a village theatre, school and public hall. It will have its own waterworks ensuring clean supply. This can be done through controlled wells and tanks."

Thus the essential logic of Gandhian economics is not only self-reliance but also self-limitation of wealth and consumption by the limit of self-labour capacity. The self-containedness of the system is built-in and complete by itself.

Facts and Faith

What do we find when we turn to facts of Indian life and some of India's aspirations embodied in its planning during twenty years (1951-71)? The village still continues to be the largest single entity in Indian economy, when thousands of villages are taken together. Industrialization so far achieved has involved only an insignificant transfer of village people from the village sector to the urban sector. In spite of this food is the most important of all problems with which India is confronted at this moment. During the fourteen year period 1951-65 food production of India recorded a substantial increase from 40 million tonnes in 1951 to about 67 million tonnes in 1965. But as population also increased at the rate of about 2 per cent per annum and the per capita money-incomes of the people increased raising demand for cereals, food-deficit of the country continued and this was made up by net import of cereals increasing from an average of 2.44 million tonnes during 1951-1955 to an average of 5.08 million tonnes during 1961-66. In 1970 it stood at a little more than 3 million tonnes.[2] It is not possible to view the question of food-import simply with reference to its economic advantage. The national policy is very much in favour of attaining self-sufficiency in food and one of the main objectives of Indian Five Year Plans is making the country self-sufficient in food. Whatever, the implication of national self-sufficiency in food in terms of economic calculus, its significance in terms of social security and welfare is too enormous to be neglected. It is simply an extension of the logic of economic self-sufficiency of a village. Indian villages would attain their economic self-sufliciency while devoting themselves to the noble task of feeding the nation adequately and properly. Looking at the world economy it is found that 60 per cent of the population in underdeveloped countries is suffering from under-nutrition or malnutrition. Economic development becomes a mockery so long as low human vitality caused by lack of proper nourishment persists extensively.[3]

Prospective Technology of the New Age

All this leads us to the fullest possible exploitation of the existing technology and, in addition, to the introduction of a technology which would vastly contribute to the improvement of efficiency of self-labour of the farming households.

Capitalism, according to Karl Marx, was destined to decay under the impact of its own inner conflict arising from accumulation of capital on the one hand and ever growing impoverishment of the masses on the other hand. This prediction was falsified. Capital accumulation and technological progress went on hand in hand. Real wages of workers went on rising. Passages from Professor Nicholas Kaldor's contribution to theory of economic growth are quoted below to depict this aspect of the evolution of capitalism.[4]

> "The historical emergence of capitalist enterprise involved a tremendous increase in the 'technical dynamism' of the economic system. The most important characteristics of capitalist business enterprise is the continuous change and improvement in the methods of production, as

> against the relatively unchanging techniques of peasant cultivation and artisan production.
>
> In the early stage of capitalist development the growth in productivity was not attended by a rise in the standard of living of the working classes. The stationery trend in real wages in Britain despite considerable improvement in production per head during the first half of the 19th century was the feature of capitalist evolution which so strongly impressed Marx and forms one of the main themes of volume one of Das Kapital. The same has been true of other capitalist countries. In the case of Japan, for instance, real wages increased very little between 1878 and 1971 despite one and a half fold increase in real income per head over the period.
>
> The second and more cheerful stage of capitalism in which production and employment continue to grow and real wages are steadily rising with the growth in production was quite unforeseen by Marx".

Fruits of technology spread throughout the period of development of capitalistic economy and reached down to the masses of workers. Technology triumphed over poverty. But even a fully developed capitalist economy is balanced on a knife-edge constantly threatened with derailment by the slightest possible disturbance. Poverty is kept far off. But there is no peace. Tensions and cold war continue with a frantic race from one position to another. Scientific resources are largely engaged in the making of high explosives and are prevented from democratizing technology for production.

In his criticism of the Marxian dialectical materialism Bertrand Russell says[5] :

> "Methods of production appear in Marx as prime causes and the reasons for which they change from time to time are left completely unexplained. As a matter of fact, methods of production change, in the main owing to intellectual causes, owing, that is to say, to scientific discoveries and inventions. Marx thinks that discoveries and inventions are made when the economic situation calls for them. This, however, is a quite unhistorical view. Why was there practically no experimental science from the time of Archimedes to the time of Leonardo? For six centuries after Archimedes the economic conditions were such as should have made scientific work easy. It was growth of science after the Renaissance that led to modern industry. This intellectual cauzation of economic processes is not adequately recognized by Marx".

Thus, if combined with a benevolent will which is certainly an essential part of humar nature, will it not be possible for science to invent a technology which would decentralize production without loss of efficiency which would enable a small farmer to have enough leisure for better planning and better management of his production and ultimately to make most effective use of his own labour power? Japan has already made some progress in this direction.

Though the Japanese economy is not modelled on the Gandhian idea of decentralization, it contains certain essential elements of a decentralized economy. A remarkable aspect of Japanese agriculture is its rapid development on the basis of small-scale farming. The phenomenal growth (nearly 70 per cent) of agricultural productivity in Japan during 1880-1930 was brought about by technological innovations which involved modest capital investments per farm and maximum utilization of farm-labour-force. Farm-mechanization in Japan developed rather slowly and initially took the form of use of small machines, e.g., electric motors, power tillers, power-sprayers, power-threshers, power-huskers, power-pumps etc. rather than big tractors. Japanese economic development provided excellent scope of combination of farm-work and industrial work.[6] This combination of farm-work and industrial work was facilitated firstly by location of a large number of important industries in the rural areas which in its turn was due to extensive development of transportation and electricity. Secondly, it was expedited by introduction of small tractors which enabled a farmer's wife and children to operate farms with week-end assistance from the family head engaged in factory occupation. Rapid adoption of garden type tractors on Japanese farms was motivated by the need for reducing the drudgery of farm-work and thereby preventing exodus of the young people from farm-work. Even the Japanese industrial structure is not dominated by big mills and machinery. Instead, it covers a "wide spectrum ranging from large scale capital-intensive enterprises to family work-shops that use little or no power machinery".[7] The illustration of the Japanese case is given here to show that a technological framework fostering decentralized production is not merely an ethical but a practical proposition. There seems to be scope of exploration of further possibilities of development along this line.

Labour is not so abundant as it appears to be

even in a country where a large part of the rural labour force remains idle during parts of the year. This is because labour, when in operation, reaches its fatigue point very soon without mechanical assistance. This is particularly true in agriculture. Is it too idyllic to set up a model for planning covering a large number of villages inter-linked to each other through townships which would be producing farm equipments, machines and other requisites by making use of a part of the rural labour force and returning these materials to agriculture for greater and more efficient production with less labour, while even this industrial part of the rural labour force continues enjoying the benefits of living in their own village homes?

Moreover, what is the rationale of the glaring distinction between manual and intellectual labour? Perhaps it is a question of finding not the rationale but facts behind the distinction. Why should not science equip even an intellectual with some small handy machines so that he is enabled to produce something of his daily consumption by exertion of his own labour? Why should not the pattern of industrial-cum-urban development be such as would make it possible for even an intellectual worker to have a plot of land along with his residence where he can produce some of his daily foods? Decentralized development of industries with an agricultural base would meet this need. Though this might cause a sacrifice of overall efficiency measured in terms of goods, it would provide for a new dimension of satisfaction measured in terms of some permanent values, e.g. beauty and peace. It is, however, national planning and not the principle of private profit-maximization which could orient economic development along this line.

Gandhiji and Rabindranath

Gandhiji and Rabindranath met on the village front. There was a remarkable affinity between the two great leaders. The social thinking of both centered on a rural-based economic development. Rabindranath did not accept *Charkha* (spinning wheel) but emphasized intensive and modernized farming as a step towards rural prosperity.[8] This difference was, however, more apparent than real. *Charkha* as a specific form of implement was less important than as a symbol of work and self-reliance. It is true that while Gandhiji emphasized austerity, Rabindranath attached more importance to aestheticism. But both were in search of outlets for creativity of men. Both of them recognized creativity as the fundamental problem of human society and subscribed to the views that it was through creativity that the aesthetic feelings of man found their expression. Society would thrive if institutions were developed to encourage creativity and curb acquisitiveness, the two being contradictory tendencies.

The highly mechanized industrial system of the modern age provides employment but does not make room for creative work. Creative work is an artistic activity which has been described by an art-specialist to be an integrating process. He says.[9]

> "Our twentieth-century existence is marked by a growing disintegration : the child is separated from his parents, the parents are separated from each other, the family members are separated from the community, labour is separated from work and further separated into parts, each compartment is again separated; science is separated from art, philosophy from religion, formal education separated into endless

> departments, the senses are separated from the intellect, and man is separated from man.
>
> Man not only needs to establish an orderly arrangement of the parts of his life, but he must integrate the parts into a meaningful whole, and the whole must become even more significant than the organization of the parts".

Art as a special branch of aesthetic activity like music or painting or writing is, however, not accessible to all. The organization of production could, however, be remodelled to introduce greater integration in the ordinary activities of man from which his livelihood is derived. The mechanical man is replaced by the creative integral man within the framework of a decentralized economy envisaged by Gandhiji. Rabindranath's conception of crafts was also a bold and sincere attempt to harmonize aesthetic needs of the mind with basic needs of the body.

A village modelled on the idea of self-sufficiency conceived by both Gandhiji and Rabindranath would not aim at insularism. It would cultivate the virtue of self-reliance for the satisfaction of essential needs but would never exclude the possibility of cooperation with outside for meeting the requirements of better and fuller living. On the other hand true cooperation or inter-dependence of the constituent units of society would grow only in complementarity with self-reliance.

It is very difficult to predict the form or course that decentralization of the national economy would take in future. Forces of centralization and decentralization are both at work. The future probably lies in a synthesis of the two tendencies. If, following Bertrand Russell, we could entertain any faith in the intellectual cauzation of historical development through scientific inventions, we could look forward to invention of a technology which would humanize man by liberating his creative energies from the enthralment of a mechanical system. The new society that would emerge from the new technological matrix would be rooted in self-reliance, personal creativity and mutual cooperation of its constituent units.

NOTES

1. Nirmal Kumar Bose, *Selections from Gandhi*, Navjivan Publishing House, 1948, pp. 70-73.
2. Indian Agriculture in Brief. Government of India, 1973, p. 118.
3. Monthly Bulletin of Agricultural Economics and Statistics, Vol. 14, July & August 1965 (F.A.O. Rome). Also, T.N. Srinivasan, 'Undernutrition: Extent and Distribution of its Incidence' in *Proceedings* of the Nineteenth International Conference of Agricultural Economists, Gower for IAAE, 1986.
4. Nicholas Kaldor, 'A Model of Economic Growth' *Economic Journal*, December 1957.
5. Bertrand Russell, Freedom and Organization (George Allen & Unwin). 1934, p. 230, quoted in Gobindachandra Mandal, *Arthanaitik Unnavan* (Book in Bengali), Firma K.L. Mukhopadhyay, Calcutta, 1974. Modern Marxists, however, believe in "self-propulsion of science". See, for example, L. Bobrov, *Grounds of Optimism*, Mir Publishers, Moscow, 1974.
6. Takekazu (Ed.), *Agricultural Development of Modern Japan* (F.A.O. Association, Japan), 1963, pp. 418, 638, 641.
7. Bruce F. Johnson, "Agricultural Development and Economic Transformation : A Comparative Study of the Japanese Experience". Food Research Institute Studies (Stanford University), November 1962, pp. 246, 248-49, 251.
8. Rabindranath Tagore, *Kalantar*, pp. 275-87.
9. D'Orcy Hayman, "Art and Man" reprinted in the American Review, October 1966, from "School Arts" May 1966

3

POSSIBILITY OF GROWTH WITH EQUITY THROUGH TRADE AND RURAL DEVELOPMENT

WHETHER ECONOMIC growth could be more consistent with equity has turned out to be a problem of great interest in recent years. The 18th International Conference of Agricultural Economists held at Jakarta (Indonesia) brought to the fore a more explicit recognition of the fact that development programmes at both national and international levels have failed to eliminate absolute poverty at least in 35 low-income developing countries. Though between 1960 and 1980 per capita GNP (Gross National Product) increased at an annual average rate of 1.7 per cent, it was still U.S. $250 only in 1981; life expectancy at birth increased by little over 20 per cent but was still 51 years in 1979 mainly because of high infant mortality, adult literacy was only 39 per cent in spite of a rise of 40 per cent during 1960-76 (B.F. Johnson and W.C. Clark).

It was felt that all was not well with the policies and programmes for growth in the Third World countries. The wrong appeared to have consisted in laying emphasis on capital-oriented rather than on consumption-oriented models (J.W. Mellor). A typical capital-oriented model was represented by the Mahalanobis model which in its turn drew its inspiration from the Harrod-Danar model of growth. The critiques of the capital-oriented models point to their neglect of human creativity in growth and the role of incentives to human contribution to development. In the early phase of development the relaxation of wage-goods-constraints and the liberalization of trade-policies to achieve this purpose could be immensely conducive to growth.

Capital-oriented programmes suffer from inequity in the growth process as they lead to indulgence in labour-saving devices best examples of which were offered by the Latin American countries (Gustav Ranis).

Taiwan set the example of promotion of labour-intensive industrial goods for export alongside the development of a more productive rural infrastructure and agricultural technology, maintaining a constancy in the inter-sectoral terms of trade. Development of small-scale rural industries in complementarity with agricultural productivity growth was the strategy of Taiwan in its initial phase of development. This was a process of growth consistent with fairer income distribution or equity.

However, in the next phase in the wake of exhaustion of surplus labour capital-intensive industrialization had to be started both for the domestic and foreign market. Room had to be made now for food-import following the emergence of savings from a highly progressive agricultural technology, releasing labour for the non-agricultural sector.

Sharply contrasted with this process, the path pursued by Columbia and the Philippines was one of import substitution in respect of skill and capital-intensive industrial goods as well as the labour-intensive primary goods. This amounted to a full-scale programme of domestic-market-oriented industrialization rooted in severe protectionism and loss of productive efficiency in appropriate output and technology-mixes. Thus while share of exports in Gross Domestic Product (GDP) was stagnating around the level of 18 per cent during the 'seventies in both Columbia and the Philippines, this was steadily rising in Taiwan (Gustav Ranis) from 30 per cent to 54 per cent. While Columbia and the Philippines lost substantially through import substitution the benefit of overall export-share in their Gross Domestic Product and savings potentiality, Taiwan's saving potentiality steadily improved through export-promotion. Some countries, in their transition from the colonial phase of primary production and export to industrialization, arrived at the phase of both import and primary export substitution.

But resort to extreme protectionism in their case has precipitated a situation of abnormal profits accruing to the indigenous capitalists at a high margin of profit with small volume of trade in a restricted home market at the cost of the possibility of larger trade at lower profit margin through export-promotion.

Taiwan is a typical example of how far appropriate trade policy could be conducive to growth with even distribution of the consequent benefits. A close co-ordination between agricultural development activities and decentralized industrialization supported by the trade-policy of export promotion enabled Taiwan to achieve a pattern of economic growth which provided her farm-households with a share of non-agricultural income to the extent of 30 per cent of their total income in 1964 rising to 52 per cent in 1972. The growth pattern in Columbia as a contrast lowered the share of non-agricultural income in total farm-income from 14 per cent to 19 per cent during the very same period. Taiwan shows how equitable growth-path fostered by labour-intensive technology in rural industrialization absorbing surplus labour of the agricultural sector yielded higher overall growth rates of the economy eventually followed by disappearance of surplus labour, causing capital-intensive production in both the agricultural and rural sectors.

Capital-oriented programmes do not necessarily result in higher growth rate or higher per capita income. Thus gross capital formation in India is 26 per cent of GNP (Gross National Product) which is higher than that of Taiwan (24%) and the same as in Indonesia. Capital-output ratio in Taiwan (1.7) and Indonesia (1.1) are appreciably lower than that in India (2.4). Yet the average annual rates of growth of GNP (1970-80) in Taiwan (8.5%) and Indonesia (7.5%) are much higher than in India (only 3.5%). Per capita annual income in Taiwan (US $2780) and Indonesia (US $530) are much higher than that in India (US $230). Much depends upon the skill of the working force in using productive resources, quality of population and the overall efficiency in the performance of the economy. The strength of organization, competence in the use of equipments and other factors, quality of management – all might combine to lower capital-output ratio in the process of growth. Possibility in this direction is more in small-scale labour-intensive units.

It is the principle of comparative advantage that imparts significance to trade-policies and practices. When one country enters into trade with other countries it enjoys a tangible benefit arising from exchange of domestic goods for foreign goods both produced at higher levels of efficiency or at lower unit costs that would not have been possible in the absence of trade.

Unfortunately, however, India's foreign trade constitutes only 12 per cent of her GNP, while foreign trade in the cases of Indonesia, South Korea, Taiwan, Philippines and Thailand constitute 49 per cent, 67 per cent, 98 per cent, 39 per cent and 47 per cent respectively of the GNP's. Per capita export of Thailand works out to US $138, while that in India is worth US $11 only. Per capita import of Thailand amounts to US $193, while India's import is worth US $20 only. It is, therefore, no wonder that the level of living in India would be much lower than that of Thailand whose per capita income is thrice as much as of India. Per capita income of the Philippines, too, though much lower than that of Taiwan is higher than that of India by 218 per cent.

However, India being a vast country with diversity of production-situations might well aspire to be a domestic market-oriented economy. She must have to go far enough toward diversification of production rather than specialization to bring her unutilized manpower and natural resources into fullest possible utilization.

But even after making an allowance for this, India is positively committed to foreign trade. And the process of industrialization had a far-reaching impact on its character. Thus the share of manufactured goods in the total volume of her exports increased from 38 per cent in 1939-40 to 48 per cent in 1953 accompanied by a decline in export of raw materials from 43 per cent to 22.7 per cent during the same period. Correspondingly the percentage of manufactured goods in the total volume of imports declined from 56 per cent in 1939-40 to 50 per cent in 1953 along with an increase in the share of raw materials in the total volume of imports from 22 per cent to 29 per cent during the same period. By 1977-78 export of manufactures and raw materials stood at 60 per cent and 13 per cent respectively of the total exports and import of raw materials shot up to 73 per cent of the total imports. It is, however, a pity that the growth of exports of manufactures was not enough to pay for bigger volume of import of consumer goods or domestic supply of consumer goods. Primarily the exports went into financing imports of machineries (19% for 1977-78) and raw materials (73% for 1977-78) for capital intensive home industries. The growth of exports as well as import of capital goods did not bring forth commensurate supply of consumer goods. Import of consumer goods had a share of 8 per cent of the total during 1977-78.

It is unfortunate for India that she did not get the benefit of superior technology of Japan delivering her cheaper and superior goods through trade as has been the case with most of the South-east Asian countries. Thus share of Japan in India's foreign trade was only 9 per cent while the corresponding shares of Japan in foreign trade of Thailand, Philippines, Malaysia and Indonesia turned out to be 19 per cent, 23 per cent, 23 per cent and 43 per cent respectively. Of course, a pattern of interregional trade relations cannot just be created at a point of time by political decisions. It is a sort of historical development arising from relative advantages, needs, resource situations and technological collaborations.

But whatever the pattern of trade-relations of India evolving in the course of a long period, there has been a qualitative change in her foreign trade. Not only has the composition of trade been radically altered as already mentioned, there has been a big change in the trade-balance. The traditional surplus has given way to chronic deficit. And the deficit went on increasing from Rs. 328 crores of 1961-62 to Rs. 905 crores of 1966-67, Rs. 977 crores of 1974-75, Rs. 1088 crores of 1978-79 and to Rs. 4109 crores of 1981-82. Moreover, the deficit was accompanied by a systematic fall in terms of trade from 100 of 1968-69 to 77 of 1974-75, 70 of 1975-76 until it stood at 90 of 1978-79. This implied that the country has not only been suffering trade-deficit but has fallen prey to a type of deficit which carried with it the sacrifice of more goods by way of export per unit of imported goods. This is a process of acute deprivation of the people, paying more in exchange of what they get in addition to bearing the growing burden of foreign debt.

It seems that there is something profoundly wrong with the working of the Indian economy. It is practically neither export-oriented, nor an effectively domestic-market-oriented economy whose aim is to provide full employment even at the cost of efficiency. The failure of the large-scale import of capital-goods to accelerate industrial productivity at a reasonable rate and the failure of Indian exports to appropriate an adequate share of foreign market possibly indicate that India has chosen a pattern of industrialization whose technical skill and capital requirements are beyond her capacity to meet. Naturally, therefore, its pace also has been too low to promote expansion of employment. This warrants that more attention be devoted to agricultural development and development of those industries which are complementary to the growth of agriculture. This might include more infrastructural development of rural sector of the economy. Even though this, too, is capital intensive, it involves use of a type of physical capital that can be abundantly produced by domestic labour with lower skill.

In this process there could be rapid expansion of

employment which in terms of growth, equity and welfare would have been highly significant. Moreover, if the policies of developed countries had rather been opposed to the export-promotion efforts of the less developed countries like India, as is alleged, intensive rural development could at least be instrumental to promoting a domestic market-oriented economy.

Recent explorations in the field of Indian agriculture have generated sufficient data to show that in those parts of the country where a high degree of agricultural growth through modern technology has been attained real wages of the workers have been higher in spite of mechanization than in other areas (Inderjit Singh, World Bank). Enhanced agricultural income has widened the scope of rural industrialization which diffuses and deepens the scientific sprit among the common rural people, overcomes their sluggishness and lays the surest foundation of economic progress without concentration of wealth in a few hands. This, too, is a path that is opposed to distortions of the economy caused by unbalanced urbanism and is more productive of social welfare

Economic growth that produces or aggravates disparity in income distribution through disproportionate shares of different social classes in additional incomes generated in the growth process is certainly less desirable than a more egalitarian model of growth. This is because the latter generates more social satisfaction than the former.

Table 3.1 shows the pattern of distribution of national income obtaining some developed and less developed countries.

TABLE 3.1: Percentage share of Household Income by percentile groups of households*

Countries	Lowest 20%	Second quintile	Third quintile	Fourth quintile	Highest 20%
India (1975-76)	7.0	9.2	13.9	20.5	49.4
Philippines (1985)	5.2	8.9	13.2	20.2	52.5
Thailand (1975-76)	5.6	9.6	13.9	21.1	49.8
Sweden (1981)	7.4	13.1	16.8	21.0	41.7
U.K. (1981)	7.0	11.5	17.0	24.8	39.7
U.S. (1980)	5.3	11.9	17.9	25.0	39.9
Germany (Federal Republic 1978)	7.9	12.5	17.0	23.1	39.5
Japan (1979)	8.7	13.2	17.5	2.1	37.5

* World Development Report, 1988, World Bank.

It is quite perceptible from Table 3.1 that social groups of lower rank in U.K., U.S., Germany (Federal Republic), Sweden and Japan are getting greater shares of National Income than their counterparts in Less Developed Countries like India, Philippines and Thailand. While the highest 20 per cent group in India, Phiippines and Thailand obtain 49.4 per cent, 52.5 per cent and 49.8 per cent respectively of National Income, the shares of highest 20 per cent group in Sweden, U.K., U.S., Germany (Federal Republic) and Japan are 41.7 per cent, 39.7 per cent, 39.9 per cent, 39.5 per cent and 37 per cent respectively. In fact, in the Developed Countries growth has been more consistent with equitable distribution of income.

How has this been possible? This is due to their more progressive social systems based on larger wage income. Though in these countries technology is highly labour-saving share of labour is not allowed to fall. Social insurance measures are a very powerful factor in ensuring reasonable share of labour.

In Less Developed Countries growth efforts are not accompanied by adequate social insurance. The high degree of inequality in India's income-distribution may be largely due to extreme poverty of the landless agricultural labourers who constitute a large proportion of the rural community. Growth of the Indian economy in consistency with equity would imply substantial rise in the wages of agricultural labour. But high wage rate may adversely affect employment offered by farmers who would resist a decline in their profit. Land is so scarce and landless agricultural labourers are so vast in number that it may not be possible to convert them into owner-cultivators through equitable distribution of land. The economic problem of agricultural labour is so vast that it calls for both national and grassroot planning for solution. Expansion of purchasing power of agricultural labour through industrial enterprises of labour cooperatives could itself provide market for their products if these are wage goods. In such a system production is brought closer to needs, eliminating possibility of market disequilibrium. There should be shift in national policy in favour of a strategy for domestic market development. This is an obvious need for a countrv like India with a huge man-power.

India's persistent trade-deficit and lowered terms of trade even in the post-1980 period particularly due to capital goods import reinforces the case for a domestic market oriented economy.[1]

NOTE

1. This chapter is based on the contributions of B.F. Johnson and W.C. Clark, J.W. Mellor, Gustav Ranis and Inderjit Singh to the 18th International Conference of Agricultural Economists, Jakarta, 24 August to 2 September 1982 in addition to the author's own findings about the Indian economy.

4

TYPES OF VILLAGES

FOR AN understanding of the potentiality of rural development it is necessary to identify the characteristics of different categories of villages. The villages may be broadly classified into three categories: progressive, less progressive and non-progressive. The gradations of progressiveness may be made in the light of empirical data on socio-economic variables by the exercise of value judgment which is a matter of social intuition.

Thus, when agriculture is the major source of livelihood for villagers, yield rate of major crop is, of course, an index of progressiveness. Other indicators may be intensity of cropping, commercialization of agriculture (evident from proportion of marketed surplus), proximity to roads and rail stations, and literacy rate. With these may be associated some other important socio-economic variables which along with the aforesaid ones reflect the pattern of rural life significantly. These other socio-economic variables may be concentration of land-ownership, extent of landlessness, population size, percentage of self-employed farm-households, labour force participation rate, number of days worked by casual agricultural labourers, percentage of irrigated land etc.

Agro-Economic Research Centres of Delhi, Madras, Visva-Bharati, Vallav Vidyanagar and Jabalpur conducted socio-economic surveys of numerous villages during 1954-1961. Biplab Dasgupta at the University of Sussex, U.K. picked up some 126 villages yielding comparable data from those villages. On the basis of 14 key socio-economic variables he classified the villages into three categories: progressive, less progressive and non-progressive as stated earlier.[1]

Following Dasgupta, the progressive villages may be interpreted as a higher stage in rural development to which non-progressive villages tend to rise. The process of development is:

(a) proletarization of poor peasantry with the increasing concentration of village resources,
(b) the shift in the mode of productions in agriculture from family-based subsistence farming to market-oriented hired-worker-based agriculture, and
(c) the increased diversification of economic and social life.

The above profile of the process of rural development, however, seems to be inconclusive for the following reasons:

(a) It lacks a measure of the pace of proletarization,
(b) The present concentration of land-ownership may not be a stable position in the face of diffusion of land-ownership under the demographic pressure dissolving households over time, and
(c) It lacks evidence of catastrophic revolutions, such as conquest of Aryans over non-Aryans, reducing the latter in vast number to mere servants who have been continuing in this position since time immemorial. They

constitute the scheduled castes and backward communities of present times. Their age-old degradation is a drag on social and cultural progress.

State intervention of modern times, however imperfect, has been persistently alleviating the intensity of misery of the underprivileged people. Conflicts and complementarity of interests have both been working side-by-side. Any study of the process of rural development is bound to be inadequate without proper appraisal of their combined effects. Resultant of the two forces is to dampen the class-contradiction. This slackens growth by moderating rental incomes and raising wage-rate. So long as private enterprise is predominant in the rural sector a strategy to strike a balance between class-incentives will need to be pursued. This will, of course, prevent growth from being spectacular.

Meanwhile, progressive villages will witness improvement of the quality of food, reduction of predominance of rice in the cropping pattern, higher degree of monetization and non-farm inputs, lower rates of interest under the influence of institutional (organized) credit and diversification of consumption. The general rate of literacy, even the rate of literacy among scheduled caste people is higher in a progressive village where percentage of schoolgoing children among both boys and girls in the age group 5-14 is higher, too.

It is true that a village which includes a group of households with large initial resource endowment will be spurred into the process of growth by their profit motive. It is also possible that the households possessing larger initial assets will get richer and richer. Whether in the wake of their growth-promoting enterprise poor will be poorer or better depends upon the absence or presence of appropriate state intervention and the growth of social infrastructure as a balancing factor. A comparative view of the pattern of income-distribution in developed and less developed countries presented in Chapter 3 shows that widening disparity may not be inevitable. On the other hand it has been seen that in a village under the impact of rapid growth of an industrial centre in the neighbourhood agriculture declined with exodus of workers unaccompanied by any compensating factor.[2]

Analysis of Dasgupta shows that percentage of self-employed agriculturist households is 33.73 per cent in progressive villages, 51.81 per cent in less progressive and 69.23 per cent in non-progressive villages.[3] Thus taken singly owner-cultivators constitute the most vital part of rural society and that they hold key position in rural development. The obvious implication is that if non-land productive inputs are placed in their hands they are likely to use them most fruitfully. Employment of rural labour largely hinges on their behaviour and incentives. It is their interests which should dominate the technological policy, because a substantial part of agricultural enterprise is in their hands.

The high degree of concentration of land resource in a progressive village, top 25 per cent of households owning 91 per cent contrasted with 62.68 per cent in a non-progressive village is likely to have attracted casual agricultural labour from outside. Higher proportion of richer agricultural households has naturally invited immigration of landless agricultural labour-households from outside. This is also responsible for much larger population in such a village. Bigger population is the result of higher agricultural enterprise due to bigger landowners. The contribution of big owner-cultivator component of the land holders to progress of the village economy must be substantial. The conventional proletarization thesis in this context needs moderation. At least the bigger population of the progressive village cannot be adequately explained by the proletarization process. It is quite possible that a part of labour force have moved from less favourably endowed non-progressive village to more favourably endowed progressive village for livelihood. And this process is long-drawn. On the whole it is not conclusively ascertained whether the difference between a progressive and non-progressive village is outcome of the process of growth or a mere structural difference coming down from generation to generation.

On the basis of data taken from village surveys carried out by the Government of India in representative villages in each of the fifteen States during 1960-62 as part of the Census of India for 1961 Irma Adelman and George Dalton arrive at some significant findings which are presented below:[4]

> "The characteristics of high income villages are a relatively high amount of land per capita, better than average performance in adopting improved agricultural technology, a large number of castes, more awareness of national social legislation and a higher than average level of educational achievement".
>
> As of 1961, the commercialization of production, better technology and better access roads, while responsible for some variance in income, were not the most important influences upon income differentials. There were probably two major reasons:

1. The technology differentials reflected in the data were largely historical differences, long in existence, and were all within the framework of traditional agriculture; and
2. The available spectrum of technology required an expensive package of complementary innovations and was not very profitable".

The quality of agricultural technology was more related to commercialization, size of village and nearness to transport facilities and town. Larger population and larger number of castes might be supposed to have been conducive to division of labour and economic welfare. Thus, formation of village types was deeply rooted in the past.

Caste system arose from racial conflicts but eventually in the form of functional division it became a stabilizing factor in society. It tempered strife through landlord-client relationship and gave scope for traditional skill. Thus, even so modern a study as that of Adelman and Dalton viewed upon number of castes as a scope of economic specialization and as a source of strength of economy in its traditional framework.[5]

However, what appeared to be a stabilizing factor turned later into a stagnating and degenerating factor to be broken through by commercialization of agriculture. The degeneration from excessive inbreeding of skill and practices was overcome by liberal intercourse with the outside world through commercialization. The larger extent of commercialization reflected in market sales of agricultural products brought farm economy into closer touch with the national economy. Thereby technologically superior inputs were brought within the reach of the farmers. "On the household budget side, cash income widens the range of choice of consumption goods, allows modern forms of savings to take place, and makes possible the purchase of services such as education, which enable people to move out of traditional village-bound culture and economy".[6]

Historical differences in village type were in the course of time modified by differences in infrastructural facilities.

Another feature of a progressive village is outmigration on the part of members of richer households who, allured by better rewards of urban areas left their village homes to take up those more lucrative occupations.[7] However, usually their link with village home was not entirely severed and they imported progressive ideas into the villages by frequent visits.

NOTES

1. Biplab Dasgupta, "A Typology of village Socio-economic system from Indian village studies", *Economic and Political Weekly*, Special Number, 1975.
2. G.C. Mandal and Associates, Economics of Rural Change, Agro-Economic Research Centre, *Visva-Bharati*, 1974, pp.42-43.
3. Biplab Dasgupta, *Ibid.*
4. Irma Adelman and George Dalton, "A Factor Analysis of Modernization in Village India", *The Economic Journal*, London, September 1971. The authors selected for their study a sample of 108 from 300 village surveys available.
5. *Ibid.*
6. *Ibid.*
7. John Connell, Biplab Dasgupta, Roy Laishley and Michel Lipton, "Migration from Rural Areas: Evidence from Village Studies", IDS, Discussion Paper No. 30, 1975.

5

THE LAND QUESTION

PRIOR TO land reforms in the post-Independence period about 50 per cent of the land area of India was under the Zamindari system accompanied by intermediary tenure holders. Though remaining 50 per cent of the lands were under the Raiyatwari system, a large proportion of the raiyats were not owner cultivators. There were many big raiyats, leasing out their lands to tillers instead of cultivating directly. The Indian nationalist movement, though centred on achievement of political Independence from foreign rule, eventually embraced progressive ideas of suitable land reforms to end inequities in the agrarian system weighed down by parasitic elements.

The aims of the land reform ideology that grew before independence under the leadership of Indian National Congress were to institute peasant proprietorship on abolition of all intermediary rights in land. To cite a case, in West Bengal prior to the abolition of estate system there were tenancy reforms during the thirties which aimed at securing fair rent, free transfer and fixity of tenure. These reforms improved the status of a tenant and virtually made him owner operator of his farm.

It was during the fifties or during the First Five Year Plan that legislation was enacted to abolish the Estate system and the intermediary tenurial rights. In Bihar such legislation was started in 1948. In

West Bengal the Estate Acquisition Act of 1953 put an end to the system of Zamindari which was introduced under Permanent Settlement Regulation of 1793. The West Bengal Estates Acquisition Act of 1953 also abolished all intermediaries between the Zamindars and cultivators. By this Act all the rights of Zamindars and tenure holders were to vest in the State. The Act also fixed upper limit of holding which was revised by West Bengal Land Reforms Acts of 1955 and 1971. In Assam the State Acquisition of Zamindaries Act was passed in 1951 which abolished all rent-receiving interests in Assam. In Orissa Tenants' Protection Act of 1948, Tenants' Relief Act of 1955 and Land Reforms Acts of 1960 were directed toward protection of interests of tenants.

In some non-zamindari areas or Raiyatwari areas ownership rights in lands in non-resumable parts were conferred on tenants. In Gujarat and Maharashtra tenants could acquire their cultivated lands by paying statutorily fixed prices. Similar provision was also made in Rajasthan. In Uttar Pradesh on abolition of intermediaries land ownership devolved on Bhumindars and Sirdars who were directly linked to the Government. In Madhya Pradesh tenants were endowed with ownership rights in non-resumable areas. These are some of the illustrations of tenants' acquiring land ownership.

The central objective of land legislation in India was to encourage owner-operation and discourage tenant farming. The purpose of owner operation was to achieve enterprise in production. The purpose of ceiling was to achieve economic and social equity.

Land-reforms have several implications:

1. Abolition of parasite landlordism in all forms.

2. Land-ownership by actual tillers.
3. Fixation of fair rent.
4. Protection of tenancy interests like those of share-croppers (Bargadars).
5. Fixation of ceiling on ownership of land.
6. Redistribution of land to secure equity.
7. Consolidation of holdings for more progressive farming.
8. Cooperative or collective farm management for securing economies of scale.

A vital part of the abolition of landlordism consists in the imposition of ceiling on extent of landownership. In the wake of imposition of ceiling the question of resumption of tenanted land for personal cultivation of a landowner came to the fore. Legislation permitted earstwhile landlords to retain certain amount of land for personal cultivation. Thus, in Andhra Pradesh a landlord could take over land for personal cultivation up to 50 per cent of the land of a tenant provided the total area of the landlord under personal cultivation including the repossessed lands does not exceed two-thirds of the ceiling area. In Punjab and Haryana the landowners are entitled to hold their land for personal cultivation up to the fixed ceiling. Similar resumption of land for personal cultivation by the landowners is permitted in Rajasthan, too. In Uttar Pradesh no resumption of leased out lands for personal cultivation by landowners is permitted. West Bengal follows more or less similar rules.

Fixation of rent was revised in almost all the States. In most States revised rent payable by tenants was between 25 per cent to 33 per cent of gross produce. Thus, the onerousness of the burden of rent was somewhat alleviated.

Land reform measures in India have shown some

obvious weakness in several ways in different parts of the country. The provision of personal cultivation might have been subject to abuse in the hands of unscrupulous landowners. It limited ownership rights of many tenants and provided large scope for non-personal cultivation by hired workers.

Fixation of ceiling was liberal in many States insofar as it was not done in consistency with capacity of a landowner for actual personal cultivation. A ceiling of 30 acres in the Punjab, 18 to 126 acres in Maharashtra, 20 to 80 acres in Orissa, 24 to 120 acres in Uttar Pradesh may be in flat contradiction with the concept of owner-operation.

In West Bengal, however, the land ceiling is socially more progressive. Initially it was fixed at 25 acres on individual holding. However, this ceiling was considered as high and lowered by an Amendment Act of 1971 (initially by an Ordinance and later by an Amendment Act of 1972). The unit of application of ceiling is a family of five members, including "husband, wife and minor children". The ceiling for such a family is 12.36 acres in areas irrigated from public sources and 17.30 acres in other areas. The principle is detailed in the Table 5.1.

Another progressive feature of land-reforms in West Bengal is the documentation with consequent tenurial security of Bargadars and the fixation of rent payable by them at 25 per cent of produce in the event of their bearing all costs of cultivation or, alternatively, at 50 per cent where all inputs are supplied by landowner. However, the Bargadars went on paying 50 per cent even after meeting all costs as a part of their regard for the age-old landlord-client relationship which has, however, been shattered in recent times by growing market consciousness of the people.

TABLE 5.1: Basis of Application of Land Ceiling

Category of person	Ceiling	
	Irrigated area	Other area
(a) A single adult or for a family with one member	2.50 hectares or 6.18 acres	3.50 hectares or 8.65 acres
(b) A family with two to five members	5.00 hectares or 12.36 acres	7.00 hectares or 17.30 acres
(c) Each person in excess of five in the case of a family with more than members	0.50 hectares or 1.24 acres	0.70 hectares or 1.73 acres
(d) A family with 9 or more members	7.00 hectares or 17.30 acres	9.80 hectares or 24.22 acres
(e) Other ryots e.g., public institutions, public trust etc.	7.00 hectares or 17.30 acres	9.88 hectares or 24.22 acres

In the absence of each holding being consolidated in one block farmers are unable to derive economies of scale and full benefits of technological improvements. It is, therefore, felt by many that consolidation of holdings could be a part of land reforms programme. The logic also applies to cooperative farming.

The presence of a vast number of landless agricultural labourers reduces all land-reform measures to insignificance. If tenant cultivators are entitled to ownership of lands, there is no ethics or logic to debar landless agricultural labourers or share croppers regularly cultivating definite plots of land from having a share in ownership of those plots. It is they who are below poverty line. Land reforms will continue to suffer from bad economics if they are not provided with means to rise above poverty line.

Though land-reforms in India apparently abolished Zamindaries land was never nationalized. It continued to remain in private hands, marking agriculture as the greatest private enterprise though fragmented in appearance. Presence of a vast number of landless workers participating in agriculture is a great anomaly, perpetuating rural poverty.

Critiques of Indian land reforms suggest that ceiling should be more stringent. Rights of tenants should receive greater measure of protection against inequitous treatment of landowners. Further, numerous uneconomic holdings have no *raison d'etre*. It is suggested that there should be a lower limit of holdings and redistribution of holdings can be successful only in the context of rural industrialization and creation of non-agricultural assets, lessening pressure upon land.

Rural industrialization can be part of a national policy of widening the domestic market by enhancing the purchasing power of poor people through rural industrialization which would create effective demand for domestic goods. They should find market even if the quality is not of high standard. Land-reforms can attain full success only when some workers quit agriculture to reduce dependence on land for livelihood, because only in that case it will be possible to constitute economic holdings.

On the other hand it is not guaranteed that owner operation by itself will enhance yield rate or overall agricultural enterprise unless the conditions are favourable from all points of view, e.g., location of holdings in compact blocks, abundance of infrastructural facilities and adequate supply of inputs, finance and marketing services. Land-reforms only remove the disincentive to enterprise but positive enterprise will be forthcoming only when the cooperant inputs, facilities and conditions are guaranteed.

Turning once more to the problem of redistribution of land it may be noted that there are economists who believe that inequity in the distribution of owned holdings may be offset by equity in the distribution of operational holdings through the process of leasing out. "I am convinced that a radical solution is not the only alternative. In pre-war Japan and Taiwan, the highly skewed distribution of land was consistent with the almost uniform distribution of operational holdings of land and the satisfactory increase in annual productivity of labour in agriculture. Steps toward institutional/ structural reforms must be taken in order to make the current highly skewed pattern of land ownership in India compatible with not-so-sharply dualistic pattern of agricultural growth".[1]

However, possibility of equity in this direction in Indian conditions requires thorough investigation. Moreover, this is a highly controversial issue as discussed in Appendix E.

NOTE

1. Hiromitsu Kaneda, "Growth with Equity in India's Agriculture in Recent Years", *Indian Journal of Agricultural Economics*, January-March 1981.

REFERENCES

Appu, P.S., "Tenancy Reform in India", in *Economic and Political Weekly*, Vol. X, Nos. 33-35, special Number, 1975.

Bose, Manjula ed., *Land Reforms in Eastern India*, Planning Forum, Jadavpur University, Calcutta, 1981.

Dasgupta, Biplab, "Sharecropping in West Bengal during the Colonial Period", *Economic and Political Weekly*, Bombay, Vol. XIX, No. 13, March 31, 1984.

Ghosh, Tushar Kanti, "Land Reforms in West Bengal: Legislation and Achievement", in Manjula Bose, ed., *Land Reforms in*

Eastern India, Planning Forum, Jadavpur University, Calcutta, 1981, pp.142-170.

Kaneda, Hiromitsu, "Growth with Equity in India's Agriculture in Recent Years", *Indian Journal of Agricultural Economics*, January-March, 1981.

Mandal, G.C. "Land Reforms in the context of Agricultural Development", *Ibid*, pp.171-182.

6

SOCIO-ECONOMIC AND CULTURAL CONDITION OF SCHEDULED CASTES AND SCHEDULED TRIBES

SINCE TIME immemorial the Indian social polity has been deeply rooted in the caste system which consisted in an elaborate hierarchy, the "depressed" and "untouchables" forming its lowest rung. At the beginning of the 'Aryans' coming to India they were characterized by three divisions, e.g., the warriors, the priests and the common people. The classes were not hardened into castes by hereditary professions or by restrictions of marriages within specific social confines. In its inception caste-formation on the basis of occupational differentiation was more a theory than a rigid practice. Casteism grew out of the emergence of *Dasas* (slaves) who were treated as outcastes.

Some how colour elements of different people struck root in the minds of the Aryans who considered the Dasas as low class because of the dark complexion of the latter.[1]

Virtually the division was between Aryans and non-Aryans. The Aryans comprised Kshatriyas (warriors), the Brahmans (priests) and Vaisyas (cultivators). The non-Aryans were Shudras. They were the same as Dasas. With the march of time variations in the characteristics of classes developed through intermixture, elevating Shudras to the rank of cultivators but still keeping them below the status of other three classes in order of piety: Migration of diverse peoples into India gave rise to diverse cultures and the caste system evolved as a means to their peaceful co-existence. In this way racial antagonism between the Aryans and aboriginals was reconciled.[2] Complexity of beliefs about people being born to inmutable status (*karma*) by virtue of deeds of past life hardened the casteism by a sanction from the priestly class which emerged as a custodian of the religious precepts of the Hindus.[3] It may be specifically noted that the disdain for dark complexion mingled with the contempt for manual labour or unclean job. According to G.S. Ghuriye the idea of purity is the keynote of casteism. He says:[4]

> "Ideas of purity whether occupational or ceremonial which are found to have been a factor in the genesis of caste are the very soul of the idea and practice of untouchability."

In fact, caste hierarchy corresponded to the hierarchy of occupational purity or dignity, any job based on manual labour being considered as despicable and classes doing manual labour as "low".

He went further in probing the matter:

> "The causes that led to the degradation of these communities are not known. We can only surmise that in addition to the ideas of ceremonial purity, which necessarily led to the despises of the occupations of these people there was perhaps the bareful influence of the belief that they were the result of miscegenation with Brahmin females".[5]

In Annals of Rural Bengal (1860) by W.W. Hunter it

is documented that early Bengal's inhabitants were composed of two elements: First were the Aryans professing to be Brahmans and second were the aboriginals who were occupying the land prior to the immigration of the Aryans. Two alternatives were open to the latter – either running away to the shelter of jungles or accepting serfdom under the Aryans.[6] The vast cleavage between the victor and the vanquished was never bridged. The divisions within the Hindu community were not merely a sort of social stratification. The division was rather in the nature of existence of two social classes separated from each other by hostility of long standing.

While four class-divisions after Manu's definition were greatly in vogue in the Central Provinces, in other parts of the country including lower Bengal only two classes, namely, Brahmins and Shudras constituted the inviolable core of the social reality.[7] The Aryans looked upon Shudras with contempt. Thus the social distance between the two classes was perpetuated. However, minute gradations among the Shudras were determined by the nature of job.

Some of the typical depressed communities (later marked as "Scheduled Castes") have been documented as follows:

Shanan, Pasi and Thiyan whose job is toddy-tapping (liquor-brewing);

Chamars, Madiga and Chakkiliyan whose job is hide and leather work;

Doms who are known as village-sweepers taking unclean food;

Mushara and Bagdi who are known as field labourers;

Rajbanshi and Namasudra who form a section of cultivators;

Doshads who are described as watchmen.

In West Bengal, particularly in the district of Birbhum Bagdis, Bauris, Mahars, Dhobas and Doms are among the important scheduled castes.

There was a great deal of resentment among the depressed communities against their social disabilities like denial of access to places of worship, public wells and educational institutions. A movement for the upliftment of the depressed communities developed along with movement for national independence. The starting of the Depressed classes Mission in Bombay by V.R. Shinde was a part of the movement of which Mahatma Gandhi himself appeared as a great champion. Dr. B.R. Ambedkar, the most outstanding leader who worked in the cause of justice for the depressed communities went so far as to advise them to join Buddhism by way of an escape from Hindu ostracism.

Some sociologists laid great emphasis on the impact of anti-caste and anti-Brahmin movement on social mobility in India, breaking through caste barriers toward promotion of wider social conglomerations. Such movement, according to them, was in process through the courses of Indian history.[8]

The Government of India Act of 1935 adopted the standardized term "Scheduled Castes' as a substitute for the wide nomenclature "untouchables," "depressed classes", "backward classes", "Harijans"[9] etc. Later Article 341 of the Constitution of the Republic of India empowered the President to notify by an order the castes, races, or tribes which shall for the purposes of the constitutions be deemed to be scheduled castes and scheduled tribes in relation to the State. The documentation of the Scheduled Castes and

Scheduled Tribes was meant for social provisions for the protection and promotion of their interests.

Special efforts to encourage education among the scheduled caste people became an integral part of the State policy. Allotment of funds to this cause went on increasing year after year. Legislation was enacted to enforce removal of several social disabilities mentioned earlier. Thus it was declared illegal to prevent scheduled caste people from entering a temple or drawing water from a public well. In addition, special privileges for the scheduled caste and scheduled tribe people, such as reservation of seats in the legislature, reservation of posts in public service etc. for them were introduced. The national pledge embodied in the Indian Constitution to abolish untouchability was thus implemented.

Some of the scheduled tribes in different States may be noted as follows : 48 tribes of Madhya Pradesh including Gond, Arrakha, Badi, Bhil, Oraon, Munda, Dhangod, Pao, Kolam, Kal etc.; 62 tribes of Orissa including Bhuiya, Bhumij Gond, Khand, Koli, Malhar, Orao, Lodha etc., 11 tribes of Meghalaya including Chakma, Garo, Khasi, Kuki, Lushai etc., Garo, Kachan, Kuki, Mikir and Naga of Nagaland; 79 tribes like Aimal, Chiru, Mao, Maring, Tang Khol, Thandon etc. of Manipur; 19 tribes like Bhil, Bhutia, Chakma, Garoo, Kalam, Khasia, Lepcha, Lushai, Kaur, Orang etc. of Tripura; 79 tribes like Bhil, Koli, Kumbi, Vhegri etc. of Gujarat; 38 tribes like Asur, Lepcha, Paiga, Khond, Hajong, Mal Pahariya, Santal etc. of West Bengal.

The Tribal people are becoming more and more conscious of their separate entities. The process of unequal development in which scheduled tribes lag behind might have inculcated in them a spirit of separation in areas of their habitation.

The legislative and administrative measures to raise the status of the scheduled caste people — failed to liberalize the attitude of the caste Hindus toward the scheduled castes. Recent times witnessed numerous cases of bloody conflicts between the two following perpetration of the atrocities by caste Hindus on the depressed class people. On the whole the relationship between the two communities continued to be devoid of friendly feeling. Of course, in West Bengal such cases of open tension were rare. But even here the relationship was not positively cordial. This was due to the class contradiction between land owners and tenants, former being generally caste Hindus and the latter scheduled castes. The mutual antipathy was rather in a dormant State.

It is quite evident that a social environment degraded and devitalised by a long tradition of domination of the superior castes over the inferior ones would frustrate all aspirations of the latter for a better life.

Indeed, a demoralised state of mind could hardly nurture the urge for improvement. This must have exercised a depressing influence on literacy and education among the scheduled caste people. One can well imagine that contempt for manual labour which breeds contempt for those whose hands are thickly soiled by manual labour could be largely defeated only by labour-saving devices in production or dirty work. Application of science and higher technology to production and other activities could go a long way toward elevating the status of toilers and sparking in them the demand for education.

The following pages will present data on some socio-economic characteristics of the scheduled caste people.

D.R. Gadgil conducted a survey of occupations

followed by heads of families in Poona in 1937. N.V. Sovani under D.R. Gadgil's leadership repeated the survey in Poona in 1954 on similar lines. The results of the two surveys of occupations of heads of families in Poona re given in Table 6.1.[10]

TABLE 6.1: Distribution of Sample Families According to Caste and Occupation in Poona per cent in occupational grade

Caste	I	II	III	IV	V	VI	VII	VIII	IX
1937									
Maratha	37.5	25.6	7.1	13.6	5.5	5.3	1.1	4.3	
Brahmin	4.8	6.0	15.0	5.7	8.5	31.3	11.3	10.1	7.4
Scheduled Caste	51.7	28.2	8.1	8.1	1.2	1.1			
Artisan I	6.3	27.0	1.5	6.3	43.1	10.3	1.5	3.9	
Artisan II	20.3	65.7	2.7	5.1	2.2	2.9		2.2	
Mali	24.2	32.7	4.6	26.8	1.9	5.2	1.3	3.3	
Weaving Caste	18.5	53.3	1.5	13.8	3.1	3.1		6.7	
Other Hindus	30.1	24.1	8.4	22.9	4.8	3.6	2.4	3.6	
1954									
Maratha	34.2	21.3	12.1	8.0	13.0	5.0	2.6	3.7	
Brahmin	4.2	5.4	12.3	3.1	15.1	27.1	17.8	5.4	7.6
Scheduled Caste	55.0	16.9	8.7	4.5	10.6	1.8			
Artisan I	6.8	11.8	1.7	5.6	53.6	9.7	4.3	5.6	
Artisan II	20.4	51.7	8.6	6.6	5.0	2.2	1.7	2.2	
Mali	30.4	23.7	3.7	20.7	13.3	2.2		5.0	
Weaving Caste	37.9	28.5	2.6	6.9	8.6	11.2	1.7	2.6	
Other Castes	21.6	16.4	6.1	17.3	10.4	5.4	7.7	9.7	2.9

(I. Unskilled manual work, II. Skilled manual work, III. Lowest profession and administrative posts, IV. Small business, V. Highly skilled and supervisory work, VI. Clerks and shop assistant, VII. Intermediate profession and administrative posts, VIII. Medium business, IX. Higher profession & salaried posts.)

Source: G.S. Ghuriye, *Caste, Class and Occupation*, Popular Book Deptt., Bombay 1961. Statement 13 and State 14, p.274 & p.276.

Some outstanding facts emerge from the figures of Table 6.1. The Brahmins (superior caste) experienced a high degree of social mobility as evident from their not being confined to their traditional occupation such as priestcraft. They were the only caste which was represented in the class of higher professions and salaried posts. On the other hand upward occupational mobility of the scheduled caste members was restricted only to the highly skilled and supervisory work. The increase of scheduled caste members in this category of occupation was probably due to industrialization in the wake of Second World War. Heads of scheduled caste families were found to be mostly occupied in the unskilled manual work. While 51.7 per cent of them were in this occupation in 1937, the percentage rose to 55 in 1954. Occupational mobility was shown somewhat more prominently in the cases of intermediate castes like Artisans, Mali and Weavers.

A more or less similar position of scheduled castes in respect of occupations can be broadly understood from Census of India 1981. Table 6.2 is related to percentage of main workers among scheduled castes and scheduled tribes in broad categories of occupations like "Cultivators", "Agricultural labourers", "Household industry (manufacturing, processing, servicing and repairs) and "other workers".

It may be seen that in every State excepting Himachal Pradesh, Jammu & Kashmir, Manipur and Meghalaya most of the scheduled caste main workers are enlisted as agricultural labourers. This is particularly true for females. Thus for West Bengal 42.66 per cent of all scheduled caste main workers and 59.59 per cent of all scheduled caste female main workers belong to the category of agricultural labourers. Out of 20 States in all except 6, the occupation of more than 50 per cent of female workers is agricultural labour.

TABLE 6.2: Percentage Distribution of Scheduled Castes Main Workers into Industrial Categories, 1981

India/State	Cultivators		Agricultural labourers		Household industry (manufacturing, processing servicing and repairs)		Other workers	
	All persons	Females	All persons	Females	All persons	Females	All persons	Females
India	28.17	16.12	42.22	68.00	3.31	3.63	20.30	12.25
Andhra Pradesh	17.41	10.39	68.24	82.70	1.41	1.15	12.94	5.76
Bihar	13.58	10.39	72.88	86.31	2.17	2.21	11.37	5.33
Gujarat	15.99	8.17	41.21	61.87	5.26	4.37	37.54	25.59
Haryana	11.86	10.91	51.28	58.23	3.56	3.05	33.30	27.81
Himachal	71.65	90.16	4.92	2.90	4.11	1.58	19.32	5.36
Jammu & Kashmir	62.79	72.28	10.05	7.72	2.01	3.50	25.15	16.50
Karnataka	27.32	13.60	46.24	65.93	2.80	3.14	23.64	17.33
Kerala	2.29	0.99	58.08	66.56	3.43	5.15	36.20	27.30
Madhya Pradesh	37.00	28.53	38.66	54.62	6.96	8.03	17.38	8.82
Maharashtra	15.63	13.22	46.84	66.06	6.18	6.35	31.15	14.37
Manipur	73.16	68.19	5.50	5.09	6.79	17.83	14.65	8.83
Meghalaya	4.58	1.70	8.12	7.34	8.07	20.34	79.23	70.62
Orissa	28.93	10.45	47.40	63.46	4.88	8.10	18.79	17.99
Punjab	6.66	1.69	60.03	51.44	3.21	4.86	30.10	42.01
Rajasthan	52.11	49.83	17.09	26.39	5.63	4.92	25.17	18.86
Sikkim	51.84	72.22	5.10	6.02	5.54	1.71	34.57	20.05
Tamil Nadu	18.18	11.27	62.98	77.75	1.33	1.34	17.81	9.61
Tripura	34.32	11.76	31.12	35.90	1.77	5.46	32.79	46.88
Uttar Pradesh	47.70	28.37	34.98	58.92	3.08	3.50	14.24	9.70
West Bengal	30.18	9.15	42.66	59.59	2.95	6.88	24.21	24.28

The picture is somewhat different for scheduled tribes (Table 6.3). In all States except 7 including West Bengal most of the main workers of scheduled tribes (more than 50%) are cultivators. The all-India average of the proportion of cultivators among scheduled tribes is 54.43 per cent, the average for the females being 43.36 per cent. This is higher in comparison with the proportion of agricultural labourers (32.67%) for all persons. However, though the proportion of agricultural labourers among females (46%) is higher than that of their male counterpart, it is lower than the proportion of female agricultural labourers among scheduled castes. In West Bengal, however, female workers among scheduled tribes are mostly agricultural labourers, forming 60.42 per cent of the total female workers (Table 6.3).

Data relating to percentages of scheduled caste and scheduled tribe persons living in rural and urban areas and percentage of scheduled caste and scheduled tribe persons to total number of persons in different States as well as for India as a whole are presented in Table 6.4.

It may be seen from Table 6.4 that percentage of scheduled caste population to total population above 20 is found only in cases of four States, namely, Himachal Pradesh, Punjab, Uttar Pradesh and West Bengal, the average percentage for all-India being 15.75. It may also be found that in all the States except Gujarat, Meghalaya and Sikkim the proportion of scheduled caste people living in rural area is greater than that in urban area.

The average percentage of scheduled tribe persons in India is 7.76. In seven States the percentage of scheduled tribe people is higher than 20. Scheduled tribe population is predominant in Meghalaya and Nagaland covering 80.58 per cent and 83.99 per cent respectively of all persons. The proportion of scheduled tribe people is considerable, covering 27.30 per cent and 28.44 per cent respectively in Manipur and Tripura. Scheduled tribe people, too, live mostly in rural areas.

TABLE 6.3: Percentage Distribution of Scheduled Tribes Main Workers into Industrial Categories

India/State	Cultivators		Agricultural labourers		Household industry (manufacturing, processing servicing and repairs)		Other workers	
	All persons	Females	All persons	Females	All persons	Females	All persons	Females
India	54.43	43.86	32.67	46.16	1.42	1.75	11.48	8.23
Andhra Pradesh	43.21	30.30	43.72	59.16	3.81	4.17	9.26	6.37
Bihar	63.06	50.17	23.20	38.51	1.80	2.00	11.94	9.32
Gujarat	45.91	32.73	40.10	58.43	0.83	0.89	13.13	7.95
Himachal Pradesh	76.91	38.01	3.58	4.16	1.19	0.62	19.32	7.21
Karnataka	40.81	23.77	40.73	61.67	2.52	3.96	15.94	10.65
Kerala	20.54	11.52	57.47	69.28	0.75	1.07	21.24	18.31
Madhya Pradesh	60.78	50.93	31.43	43.30	0.97	1.02	6.87	4.75
Maharashtra	39.53	34.37	45.22	57.05	2.00	1.97	13.25	6.61
Manipur	86.30	92.77	2.71	2.65	0.76	1.17	10.77	3.41
Meghalaya	69.55	72.31	9.97	10.38	0.63	0.88	19.85	16.43
Nagaland	83.86	94.99	0.31	0.18	0.23	0.27	15.60	4.56
Orissa	52.15	29.24	36.21	57.52	1.43	2.70	10.21	10.54
Rajasthan	78.05	61.91	9.87	24.07	0.24	0.34	11.84	13.68
Sikkim	66.45	76.68	1.85	1.54	0.86	1.28	30.74	20.54
Tamil Nadu	47.33	38.13	34.03	45.75	1.67	1.78	17.02	14.34
Tripura	64.03	55.83	28.72	37.80	0.24	0.51	7.01	5.86
Uttar Pradesh	78.74	76.24	7.22	7.58	4.85	11.76	5.19	4.42
West Bengal	31.04	18.44	48.73	60.42	1.05	1.43	19.08	19.71

The data of Table 6.4 can be interpreted to signify that urban industrialization or tertiary development in urban areas has offered little job opportunities to scheduled caste or scheduled tribe male or female workers. This is particularly true for West Bengal.

Data relating to rates of literacy among total population and among scheduled caste and scheduled tribe population are presented in Table 6.5 and Table 6.6 respectively.

TABLE 6.4: Percentage of Members of Scheduled Castes and Scheduled Tribes Population in Total, Rural and Urban Areas, 1981

India/State	Scheduled Castes			Scheduled Tribes		
	Total	Rural	Urban	Total	Rural	Urban
India	15.75	17.34	10.63	7.76	9.54	2.03
Andhra Pradesh	14.87	16.44	9.68	5.93	7.25	1.53
Bihar	14.51	15.17	9.86	8.31	8.90	4.15
Gujarat	7.15	6.99	7.57	14.22	19.13	3.35
Haryana	19.07	20.79	13.12			
Himachal Pradesh	24.62	25.22	17.34	4.61	4.91	0.96
Jammu & Kashmir	8.31	9.31	4.55			
Karnataka	15.07	16.54	11.43	4.91	6.02	2.19
Kerala	10.02	14.52	12.45	22.97	27.78	0.11
Madhya Pradesh	14.10	14.52	12.45	22.97	27.78	4.10
Maharashtra	7.11	7.52	6.43	9.19	12.67	2.15
Manipur	1.25	1.42	0.79	27.30	32.79	12.05
Meghalaya	0.41	0.27	1.05	80.58	86.13	51.03
Nagaland				83.99	89.70	57.91
Orissa	14.66	15.06	11.68	22.43	24.26	8.77
Punjab	26.87	30.20	18.19			
Rajasthan	17.01	17.71	14.54	12.21	14.89	2.16
Sikkim	5.78	5.41	7.67	23.27	23.60	21.54
Tamil Nadu	18.35	21.85	11.23	1.07	1.45	0.32
Tripura	15.12	15.91	8.67	28.44	31.53	3.40
Uttar Pradesh	21.16	23.09	12.33	0.21	0.24	0.06
West Bengal	21.99	26.19	10.31	5.63	7.36	0.80

Table 6.5 shows that the general rate of literacy is lowest in Rajasthan (24.38%), female literates being only 11.42 per cent. The general rate of literacy is highest in Kerala (70.42%) where even the female literacy rate is as high as 65.73 per cent. The

average Indian rate of literacy is 36.73 per cent; the excess of male literacy rate over female is about 22. West Bengal occupies 8th place in respect of literacy, scoring 40.91 per cent of literates. But the excess of male over female rates of literacy is about 20. The excess of male literacy rate over female rate is highest (about 25) in Rajasthan and Lowest (about 9) in Kerala. Thus, comparatively lower rate of female literacy is a factor which tends to depress the general rate of literacy.

TABLE 6.5: Literacy Rates among Total Population, 1981 (The percentages of literates to total population in India and the States including the 0-1 age group)

India/State	Persons	Male	Female
India	36.23	46.89	24.82
Andhra Pradesh	29.94	39.26	20.39
Bihar	26.20	38.11	13.62
Gujarat	43.70	54.44	32.30
Haryana	36.14	48.20	22.27
Himachal Pradesh	42.48	53.19	31.46
Jammu & Kashmir	26.67	36.29	15.88
Karnataka	38.46	48.81	27.71
Kerala	70.42	75.26	65.73
Madhya Pradesh	27.87	39.49	15.53
Maharashtra	47.18	58.79	34.79
Manipur	41.35	53.29	29.06
Meghalaya	34.08	37.89	30.08
Orissa	31.23	47.10	21.12
Punjab	40.86	47.16	33.69
Sikkim	34.05	43.95	22.20
Tamil Nadu	46.76	58.26	34.99
Tripura	42.12	51.70	32.00
Uttar Pradesh	27.16	38.76	14.04
West Bengal	40.91	50.67	30.25

Lowest rate of literacy (10.40%) among scheduled caste people is experienced by Bihar where among those people the female rate of literacy is deplorably low (2.51%). Kerala scores the highest rate of literacy among the scheduled caste people (55.96%), female rate of literacy being 49.73 per cent. The Indian average rate of literacy among scheduled caste people is 21.38 per cent. In West Bengal it is 24.37 per cent. The excess of male rate of literacy over the female rate among the scheduled caste people is almost the same (20) for West Bengal and India as a whole (Table 6.6).

Among scheduled tribe people (Table 6.6) the lowest rate of literacy (7.8%) is found in Madhya Pradesh and highest in Nagaland (40.32%). The Indian average rate of literacy among scheduled tribe people is 16.35 per cent which is higher than the West Bengal rate by 3. The rate of literacy among scheduled tribe people is lower than that among scheduled caste people. In all cases it is found that the female rate of literacy is lagging behind the male rate, thus dragging down the average rate of literacy. These data highlight special character of the problem of literacy among scheduled caste and scheduled tribe people, particularly among their female members. Eventually these people who are basically non-Aryans in origin. were downcast in relation to the Aryans and destined to servility from generation to generation. This aspect of their life calls for tremendous efforts to kindle in their heart the spirit of learning and progress.

TABLE 6.6: Literacy Rates 1981 (The percentages of literates to total population among scheduled castes and scheduled tribes in India and the States including the 0-1 age group)

India/State	Scheduled Castes			Scheduled Tribes		
	Persons	Male	Female	Persons	Male	Female
India	21.38	31.12	10.93	16.35	21.52	8.04
Andhra Pradesh	17.65	24.82	10.26	7.82	12.02	3.46
Bihar	10.40	18.02	2.51	16.99	26.17	7.75
Gujarat	39.79	53.14	25.61	21.14	30.41	11.64
Haryana	20.15	31.45	7.06			
Himachal Pradesh	31.50	41.94	20.63	25.93	38.75	12.82
Jammu & Kashmir	22.41	32.31	11.70			
Karnataka	20.59	29.35	11.55	20.11	29.96	10.03
Kerala	55.96	62.33	49.73	31.79	37.52	26.02
Madhya Pradesh	18.97	36.26	6.87	10.68	17.74	3.60
Maharashtra	35.55	48.85	21.53	22.29	32.28	11.94
Manipur	33.63	42.94	24.95	39.74	48.88	30.35
Meghalaya	25.78	33.28	16.30	31.55	34.19	28.91
Nagaland				40.32	47.32	32.09
Orissa	22.41	35.26	9.40	13.96	23.27	4.76
Punjab	23.86	30.96	15.60			
Rajasthan	14.04	24.40	2.69			
Sikkim	28.06	35.74	19.65	10.27	18.85	1.20
Tamil Nadu	29.67	40.65	18.17	20.46	26.71	14.00
Tripura	33.89	43.92	23.24	23.07	31.22	8.69
Uttar Pradesh	14.96	24.83	3.90	20.45	31.22	8.69
West Bengal	24.37	34.26	13.70	13.21	21.16	5.01

NOTES

1. Romila Thapar, *A History of India*, Vol. I, Penguin Books, 1977, pp.37-38.
2. Herbert Risley, *The People of India*, Oriental Books Reprint Corporation, Delhi, 1969, p.262.
3. *Ibid.*, p.375 and also J.H. Hutton, *Caste in India*, Oxford University Press, Bombay, 1969.
4. G.S. Ghurye, *Caste and Race in India*, Popular Prakashan, Bombay, 1979, p.307.
5. *Ibid.*, p.313.

6. W.W. Hunter, Annals of Rural Bengal (*Gram Banglar Itikatha*, translation from English into Bengali by Ashim Chattopadhyay), Subarna Rekha, Calcutta, 1984, p.68.
7. W.W. Hunter, *op.cit.*
8. See, for example, M.N. Srinivas, Future of Indian Caste, *Economic and Political Weekly*, Vol. XIV, Nos. 7 & 8, Annual Number, 1979.
9. 'Harijan' was the name given by Mahatma Gandhi to denote the untouchable classes.
10. Cited in G.S. Ghuriye, *Caste, Class and Occupation*, Popular Book Depot, Bombay 1961, Statement 13 and Statement 14, p.274 and p.276.

7

RURAL CREDIT

FROM TIME immemorial money-lending or usury has been recognized as a regular profession.

In India private money-lending is supposed to be associated with rural poverty which arose from gradual expropriation of the poor peasants and the passing of their lands into the hands of jotedars and substantial farmers who in this process emerged as a class combining money-lending with landlordism and farming. Money-lending business, grew into a perpetual feature of the semi-feudal society and tightened its grip on the rural poor converted into tenants or farm servants. Though extensive data are not available showing how far impoverishment of peasants was due to the process of land transfer and how far due to the long persistent inequitable distribution of land, rural poverty is an incorrigible fact which facilitated the domination of landlordism and usurious capital.[1]

The process seems to have been accentuated by agrarian structure characterized by a highly skewed distribution of holdings and landlord-tenant relationship.

Past studies were almost unanimous about the severity of the terms and conditions of which credit was offered by the rural money-lenders irrespective of whether they were called *Bunneah* or Mahajan.[2] The exorbitant rates of interest and the methods by which repayments were exacted went on adding to the burden of rural indebtedness that assumed great importance in Indian rural studies. The seriousness of the problem also evoked legislative measures for regulating the private money-lending business and rationalizing the terms and conditions of rural credit.

Interactions between the private money-lending practice, socio-political movements and the growth of productive potential including institutional finance opened up new possibilities of significant development in the rural credit scene.

One could form a definite idea about the magnitude, nature and pattern of rural credit from the All India Rural Credit Survey of 1951-52 conducted by a Committee of Direction appointed by the Reserve Bank of India. The survey revealed that cooperative credit institutions played an almost insignificant role in extending credit to the agriculturists. In 1951-52 only about 3 per cent of the total credit needs of the rural families were met by them. Governmental agencies supplied an equal proportion and commercial banks supplied only one per cent. The rest of the credit needs were met by private money-lenders. About 25 per cent of the total credit needs for rural families came from the agriculturists. Professional money-lenders supplied about 44 per cent. About 14 per cent came from relatives, traders supplied about 6 per cent. Other agencies supplied only 1.8 per cent. Thus taken singly professional money-lenders were the biggest of the informal credit agencies. In West Bengal the picture was a little different. Here professional money-lenders were found to be more important, extending about 59 per cent to rural families. Next in importance was the role of relatives who supplied about 33 per cent of the loans. The share of agriculturist money-lenders was insignificant (2 per cent).

All India picture shows that major part of the loans were meant for consumption. Loans taken from private money-lenders were mostly for consumption. According to the All India Debt and Investment Survey of 1971-72 conducted by the Reserve Bank of India, share of institutional finance in the total debt of the cultivators was 31.7 per cent; the remaining 68.3 per cent came from non-institutional agencies.

A big change in the rural credit scene was, however, reported by the All India Debt and Investment Survey of 1981-82. According to this survey the share of institutional finance in total rural credit sharply rose from 31.7 per cent to 63.3 per cent, reducing the contribution of non-institutional agencies to 36.7 per cent.[3] Almost similar was the finding of the National Sample Survey, the share of institutional finance rising from 29.2 per cent of 1971 to 61.2 per cent of 1981 accompanied by a fall in the share of non-institutional credit from 70.3 per cent to 38.8 per cent during the same period.[4]

However, the distribution of institutional credit among asset-holders of different size-groups was far from being equitable. Thus, holders of assets up to value of Rs. 1000 obtained only 8.9 per cent of their total amount of credit from institutional sources, the rest 91.1 per cent being supplied by non-institutional agencies. Share of institutional credit in the total borrowings of asset-group Rs. 20,000 –50,000 was 55.1 per cent, non-institutional sources claiming only 44.9 per cent. The average share of institutional credit in the total credit of all asset-groups was as big as 61.2 per cent, share of non-institutional credit being 38.8 per cent only. Thus, it is quite evident that distribution[5] of institutional credit was heavily biased in favour of large asset holders.

Indications of Changes in Rural Credit Scene: A Case Study

Indeed, progress of institutional finance might arouse expectations of its far reaching impact on rural credit. A NABARD-research Project entitled "Understanding Rural Money-lenders in West Bengal" conducted by the Agro-Economic Research Centre at Visva-Bharati in 1986 revealed some facts of fundamental significance. Though the study was limited to rural households of only two villages in the district of Birbhum not far from Santiniketan, its findings might have wider implications beyond their confines about future credit possibilities in the process of rural development. The lessons of the findings might apply to other areas, too, where similar conditions prevailed.

One of the village under study was more advanced than the other. The advanced village was characterized by greater degree of dependence on non-agricultural occupations and was more market oriented in comparison with the less advanced village. In the former village the proportion of foodgrain output sold in market was much greater than in the latter.

The study could not trace any professional money-lender in any of the villages. In fact, in the informal credit sector money-lending was combined with other occupations of the lenders.

Predominant explicit rate of interest for informal sector in both the categories of villages was found to be zero, covering 51 per cent of loan cases in the backward village and 46 per cent in the advanced village. Predominant supplier of interest-free informal sector credit in both the villages was trader. Next important supplier of interest-free credit was owner cultivator in the backward village and service-holder in the advanced. Next predominant explicit rate of interest for informal sector loans was 50 per cent (irrespective of time). This was found in the backward village but not in the advanced one. In the backward village predominant supplier of informal sector credit bearing 50 per cent rate of interest was owner cultivator, offering about 94 per cent of the loans. Predominant classes of recipients of interest-free informal-sector-loans were owner cultivators in both the villages, obtaining loans primarily from traders. Next important recipient of interest-free informal sector loans was tenant cultivators, primarily receiving the loans from owner cultivators in the backward village and to a large extent from service-holders in the advanced village. Predominant recipients of informal sector loans, bearing 50 per cent rate of interest are tenant cultivators in the backward village. There were no such loan cases in the advanced village.

A large part of interest-free informal sector loans was offered to cultivators by traders as advances according to a forward contract which bound the former to sell paddy to the latter at the harvest price immediately after harvest. Contract-bound sale of paddy was 87 per cent in the backward village and 99 per cent in the advanced. Traders' gain from such advances consisted in sale at a higher price later.

Most of the informal sector loans was offered against intangible collateral. Intangible collateral was represented by personal qualities like long-standing familiarity, working ability, friendly relations etc. of debtors. A high degree of acceptance of intangible collateral and near-absence of tangible collateral implied easy situation of informal sector credit.

Extent of default cases of informal sector loans

was much less (6.47 per cent of amount borrowed in the backward village, 17.16 per cent of amount borrowed in the advanced village) than those for formal sector loans (18.48 per cent of amount borrowed in the backward village, 26.21 per cent of amount borrowed in the advanced village).

Borrowers were required to wait for more than a month to obtain a formal sector loan in 60 per cent of cases in the backward village and 55 per cent in the advanced village. Informal sector loans were reported to be offered instantaneously in 65 per cent of cases in the backward village and 96 per cent of cases in the advanced village.

Most common reason of special preference for informal lender is long-standing familiarity of the borrower with the lender. As distinguished from formal credit, informal credit offered by owner cultivators was supposed to have a unique character of its own consisting in instantaneous availability irrespective of purpose at the moment of emergency or at the most appropriate time of need against intangible collateral like "long-standing familiarity" of borrowers with creditors. Moreover, informal credit sector specialized in consumption or subsistence credit which was rather neglected by the formal or organized sector. All these special attributes of informal sector credit enabled it to face competition of institutional (formal) credit in spite of lower interest-charge of formal sector.

Interest-free credit offered by owner-cultivators to tenants or offered by traders to cultivators was reported to carry some implicit interest in the form of labour services at wage rate lower than the market rate in addition to ensuring future supply of labour at a critical time of operation. Interest-free credit made available by traders to cultivator sellers of their product (paddy) is part of a forward contract by which supply of product just after harvest at a harvest-time low price is guaranteed. On the whole, interest-free credit and credit bearing 50 per cent rate of interest appear to be inherent in owner-tenant relations of production or trader-cultivator relations of transactions. It seems that consumption is the major determinant of demand for loans, while supply of loans is determined by creditors' socio-economic relations with debtors.

Subsistence was found to be continuing as a major force underlying the determination of demand for loan support of which is reduced to an integral part of the socio-economic relations of the system of production and marketing transactions.

A paper showing relationship between consumption-borrowing and rates of interest establishes a high degree of correlation (0.79) between the two.[6] It was felt that until technological forces, economic development and social reforms are strong enough to overcome the subsistence pressure on the economy, informal credit would continue to occupy a substantial part of the rural credit system.

The continuation of informal credit is rationalized by its functional integration with labour services of debtors and marketing or other services of creditors. This is conspicuously absent in the case of institutional credit. If the organized credit system makes more liberal provision for consumption loan or production loan payable to labour and emergency credit, exclusive dependence on informal sector for subsistence or emergency loan may be lessened. Rapid sanction and disbursement of loans, relaxation of the requirements of material collateral and closer touch of officials with customers might further popularize institutional credit as an alternative to informal sector credit. The scope of production oriented rural credit would be widened only when the rural economy is raized beyond subsistence limit by development efforts.

The case study does not lend support to the concept of ruthless and naked exploitation of rural money-lenders. The penetration of institutional credit to the extent of 48 per cent and 50 per cent respectively into the advanced and less advanced village might have been one of the factors among others which exercised a liberalizing influence on the role of private creditors. Other factors may be identified as follows:[7]

1. The pressure of socio-political movement in West Bengal.
2. Opening of new horizon in agricultural production through technological innovations.
3. A higher degree of appreciation of the services of labourer-debtors by land-owner-creditors in the new technological situation.

However, there is still further scope of development towards reduction of the subsistence pressure on rural credit.

NOTES

1. Amit Bhaduri, *Economic Structure of Backward Agriculture*, Academic Press, London, 1983.
2. Among numerous studies on the subject references may be specifically made to Pradhan H. Prasad, "Reactionary Role of Usurers Capital in Rural India", *Economic and Political Weekly*, Vol. IX, No. 13, 1974; All India Rural Credit Survey (1951-52), Reserve Bank of India and Amit Bhaduri. *Economic Structure of Backward Agriculture*, 1983.
3. Reserve Bank of India, All India Debt and Investment Survey 1981-82, Bombay, 1986.
4. 26th and 37th Round of National Sample Survey, Report No. 322, 1985 quoted in T. Haque and Sunita Verma,

"Regional and Class Disparities in the Flow of Agricultural Credit in India", *Indian Journal of Agricultural Economics*, Vol. XLIII, No. 3, July-September, 1988.

5. *Ibid.*
6. Dr. G.C. Mandal, "Past Documentations of Rural Credit in India and their Future Implications" — paper presented at the discussion meeting on NABARD Research Project "Understanding Rural Money-lenders in West Bengal" held on 31.1.86 at the Agro-Economic Research Centre, Visva-Bharati.
7. For an elaborate account of the liberalising impact of development on money-lender interest, see Farrukh Iqbal, "The Determinants of Money-lender Interest Rates: Evidence from Rural India", *The Journal of Development Studies*, Vol. 24, No. 3, 1988.

8

DECENTRALIZED PLANNING

DECENTRALIZED PLANNING has at least three implications: One is devolution of authority from centre to lower bodies in the hierarchy of administration. The devolution applies both to decision-making and execution.

The second implication is decentralized allocation of funds to different territorial areas composing the country. According to this principle finance is more or less equitably distributed over all areas or administrative districts.

The third implication is decentralization of development projects instead of their concentration in and around big cities or a few select areas. It is the third implication of developmental planning which is of great concern in the present chapter of the book and its practical aspect is highly important. It may not be exaggerated if it is stated that the essence of decentralized planning lies in area-approach to development.

In a wider perspective area development programme has several aspects which may be neglected in an official Area Development Programme that is found in practice. First of all, the concept of area-approach to development emerges from the basic fact that areas differ from each other in respect of socio-economic characteristics and development requirements. Area development would, therefore, naturally involve identification of different areas according to their specific resources, demographic and ecological conditions, the level of utilization of the resources and level of prosperity or poverty.

Area development is closely allied to Community Development in sofar as the latter lays special emphasis on local resources. A Community Development Programme was supposed to be instrumental to the pooling of village resources for the construction of social overheads in the villages. It was expected to establish a link between an economic project and the local people and show how collective action could expedite its fruitful execution. It was expected to produce a cultural regeneration among the local people through intensive educational efforts centering around the specific projects of a Community Development Block. It led to the creation of local units for development planning.

Community Development Programmes, however, did not attain the expected success because of their deficiency in technological content and provision of infrastructural facilities and their inability to evolve area-oriented projects to make best possible use of the local human resources. Moreover, voluntary labour could not be effective among a poverty-stricken famished population. Perhaps some constructional activities at a wage below the market wage rate could be planned to arouse the enthusiasm of people if such activities could be closely linked to their actual needs. But such dovetailing never materialized. Class and caste divisions stood in the way. Wrong conception of idle labour led to overestimation of cheap supply of labour for the construction of social overheads. The incorrectness of the concept was abundantly proved by utter failure of efforts to utilize "idle" labour at lower wages.

The idea of area-specific projects brings us to the problem of proper identification of a planning area. The identification of a planning area may be guided by the identification of its peculiar resources, problems and needs. At least two criteria can be followed simultaneously in the demarcation of planning areas: one is the criterion of self-sufficiency in respect of resources and sustained growth and the other is the criterion of overall economic level already attained by an area.

The criterion of self-sufficiency means coherence of the area in view assured by a network of communications holding closely together its constituent parts. The compactness of the area assumes mobility of inputs of production between one part and another. Since the compactness of the entire territory of a country may not be feasible the division of the country or a State into a number of compact areas has a special significance from the development point of view. It means that when a project area is coterminous with a well-defined compact area the resources lying within it are put to the best possible use. There is little wastage in the form of unnecessary transportation of resources. The size of the planning area is determined by compactness and self-sufficiency. Thus the criterion would have three implications: speciality of resources, size of territory and compactness of area determined by locus of activities.

Overall economic level may be considered as another criterion for the determination of planning areas. Thus, economically backward areas in regard to per capita income and poor level of utilization of resources may be identified for special developmental planning.

Since Indian national plans are greatly concerned

with the removal of poverty and the fulfilment of minimum needs of the masses of people mostly living in rural areas, an important step toward the objective would be a thorough and complete identification of the poor zones of the country. When this has been done, a complete survey of the peculiar problems, resources, needs and possibilities of those areas should be carried out. On the basis of data emerging from these surveys area-specific development programmes may be launched in those areas. If there is any thing like rural unemployment or under employment it can be specifically located in these poor semi-arid zones. These zones are sharply different from irrigated multiple cropped areas where unemployment or underemployment is least. Thus the development of backward areas would contribute to a rapid rise in the economic level of people below poverty line.

What will then be our priority in regard to the selection of areas for development planning? Should the order of priority be: advanced areas first, backward areas later? Argument for attaching top priorities to advanced areas is rapid generation of surplus to be available for investment in backward areas in a later period. This was the consideration for prior selections of progressive areas in the Comprehensive Area Development Programme of West Bengal. The Comprehensive Area Development envisaged centres for supply of inputs and technical services to ensure intensive utilization of land resource for multiple cropping and substantial increase of income from improved animal husbandry. There were also plans for the development of small industries to provide additional or alternative sources of income. But while prior selection of advanced areas for CADP was too forceful to be neglected, it was apprehended that backward areas might be kept waiting for unduly long period for their turn. As a counter to this hazard, consideration could be given to the possibility of establishing linkage of a backward zone with nearest CADP block of highest development potentiality. The determination of the exact form of the linkage would form part of planning under Comprehensive Area Development Programme. The linkage would be a medium of transmission of multiplier and accelerator of heavy investments in CADP blocks to the nearest backward zones. The question of immediate upliftment of the backward areas from the point of view of the fulfilment of minimum needs of people could be fitted into the model for surplus generation in more advanced areas by suitable organization, communications transportation systems, planning and administration.

The most important indicators that would guide delineation of a planning area are as follows:

(a) Pattern of natural resources including types of land irrigated and unirrigated,
(b) Pattern of demography,
(c) Density of population,
(d) Pattern of enterprises and occupations,
(e) Per capita income,
(f) Cropping pattern,
(g) Inputs and outputs for enterprises,
(h) Prices and wage rates, and
(i) Communications,

Types of villages reviewed earlier in Chapter 4 may be fitted into the demarcation of planning areas.

When broad areas have been delineated in accordance with the above noted indicators, it is possible to divide these areas further into sub-areas.[1] An economic sub-area may be determined broadly with reference to the possibility of completeness in terms of economic activities as part of the areas held together in a hierarchy of central places, such as village level trading centres run by retail sellers and agents buying farm products from individual farm households, centres of intermediary traders and wholesale trading centres. Most rudimentary necessities of daily life are bought and sold at the village level shopping centre. A little more uncommon goods are available at the intermediary trading centres where also village level retailers make their purchases. Then comes the wholesale trading centres which supply goods to the intermediary trading centres, undertake processing and import from and export to other areas. Sub-areas contained in the system of three-tier hierarchy may be considered as parts of the bigger planning area defined in terms of a number of indicators stated above. These are small areas whose components have a degree of integration and which share in highest degree of movement or inter-communications of people and resources within their ambit. It is vital to the problem of rural development to identify such small loci of economic activities.

An alternative conception of four-tier growth foci comprises (1) Service centres, (2) growth points at the sub-regional level, (3) growth centres at the regional level, and (4) growth poles at the national level.[2]

Function of a service centre is to meet some elemental needs of people living in a number of villages around the centre. It has potentiality to serve as a centre for diffusion of urban influences and initiate the process of urbanization. Growth points are the same as market towns serving about 300 villages consisting of 10 to 20 service points.

Growth points will be mostly agro-industrial, their main function being processing agricultural and dairy products. For 5 to 10 growth points there will be a growth centre whose function will be to serve as industrial hubs of its area, meeting regional needs of inputs and services and consuming agricultural products. Their structure should be such as will be capable of generating external economies to facilitate big or medium sized industrial production. Growth poles will be at the apex of the hierarchy, functioning as national centres of finance, technology and research giving nourishment to all growth points.

It should be an integral part of national planning to dispel congestion of big cities and stimulate development of service centres and market towns that will strengthen the rural economy.

In essence the area-approach imparts a new significance to development planning. It facilitates adaptation of planning to specific problems of different areas. It leads to decentralization of investment programmes based on a new ordering of economic processes. It provides a framework for harmonizing micro- and macro-plannings. The objective of rural development planning should be to bring about fuller utilization of the local resources bv making arrangements for the supply of cooperant inputs. The local deficiencies in respect of supply of inputs should be estimated beforehand and arrangements made to make up the deficiencies. These inputs do not simply consist of material goods, such as fertilizers, equipments and machines but also services and facilities, such as credit, marketing and technical services.

The central points of sub-areas are expected to function as centres of rural development. They are expected to develop as the location of industries, technology and services which would contribute to agricultural and rural development. They are expected to establish best possible conditions of rural development by producing a relationship of complementarity between rural and industrial development. While they draw upon the farm product-supplies of the villages as inputs for industries, they in their turn are expected to bring within the reach of the villages all the requisites of scientific production and civilized life. They could contribute to community asset formation in the neighbouring villages by supplying to them at moderate cost requisites of communications, sanitation, electrification and housing materials. Thus these centres would ensure an all-round development of the village economy and a substantial improvement of the level of living of the rural population.[3]

Gram Panchayat, the primary unit of self-government at the village level has great potentiality as an instrument of decentralized planning. It would serve as a link of popular experience with the technical assessment of local resources, entrepreneurship for their utilization and market for the products. Combination of popular experience and techno-business enterprise could well become a powerful engine of progress.

The revival of Panchayats in recent years is in keeping with the tradition of highly decentralized and pluralistic constitution of Indian society even under monarchic or oligarchic rule. Much of the functions of the authority in the past were delegated to the local associations. Thus, it is in the fitness of things that the local bodies would be involved in local planning. Participation of local bodies in identification and utilization of local resources would be a great step forward for developmental planning and removal of poverty. An all party approach to local level planning and development would be all the more desirable to achieve this laudable objective. Developmental objectives are lost amidst party conflicts and social tensions. Hence, within the framework of Parliamentary democracy making room for party-contests at higher levels, there should be unified approach to the solution of local issues.

In this connection the role of voluntary associations deserves serious consideration. What is or what should be the peculiar role of voluntary associations in rural development when there are so many professional or official organizations concerned with the task? Of course, at the grass root level voluntary associations fulfil or are supposed to fulfil a task which official agencies cannot cope with. Then, the question is: Who will form a voluntary agency? Will it be an association of the beneficiary workers or some enlightened and public spirited persons. If it is a body composed of beneficiaries having common interest then it becomes a cooperative society whose domain is wide. Chapter 9 discusses its objectives, development, constitution and functions. If it is a social service agency, then its composition must be one of persons having missionary devotion to the cause of the rural beneficiaries. They may be retired persons ready to offer service without any remuneration or with a remuneration much lower than the normal. Or they may be persons still in service but ready to spend a part of their time for the rural cause without any remuneration or they may be students inspired with the idea of social service. A great merit in their case is naturally low administrative cost.

All India picture presents illustration of such voluntary associations as Maliwada Human

Development Project, Aurangabad, Maharashtra; Social work and Research Centre and Rural University Jawja Rajasthan; Gandhi Vichar Parisad, Action Research Institute, Weavers' Cooperative Societies in the district of Bankura, Khelaghar in the district of N-24 Parganas in West Bengal and many others.[4]

Involvement of these associations in running production cum training centres in diverse fields is appreciable. The activities comprise production in the fields of handloom weaving, poultry, herbal medicine, gloves for steel workers, leather goods, batik prints, tailoring, spices, fruit-processing etc.

If the voluntary associations work with missionary zeal they can render invaluable service to the upliftment of rural economy in the following forms by virtue of their close touch with the people.

1. Triggering cultural revolution in favour of manual work.
2. Generating appropriate motivation of people for innovations in techniques of production.
3. Bringing knowledge within the reach of people about production of new things.
4. Generating demand for sanitation, health care, family planning, hygienic practices and more nutritive food.

Thus voluntary associations are expected to be highly useful in decentralized planning because of their living in close proximity to the rural people.

NOTES

1. Out of the growing volume of literature on the subject a few contributions are noted here:

(a) Karl A. Fox and T.K. Kumar, "Dilineating Functional Economic Areas".
(b) Brian I.L. Berry, "Reflections on the Functional Economic Areas".
(c) E.L. Baun and R.G. Speigelman, "Two Suggested Critical Topics for Research", all published in the collective volume Research and Education for Regional and Area Development, IOWA State University Press, 1966.

2. R.P. Misra, "Growth Poles and Growth Centres in the context of India's Urban and Regional Development Problems" in Antoni Kulinski, ed. *Growth Poles and Growth Centres*, United Nations Research Institute for Social Development, Geneva (Mouton, Paris).
3. G.C. Mandal, "The Role of Area-approach in Agricultural Development and the Removal of Rural Poverty", *Economic Affairs*, Calcutta, June-July, 1974.
4. See NABARD Study of the Non-farm Sector, Agro-Economic Research Centre, Visva-Bharati, (Unpublished), 1990.

9

THE ROLE OF COOPERATIVES

A COOPERATIVE may be defined as a voluntary and legal organization constituted on the basis of the principle of mutual aid to serve common interests of the people concerned. It is instrumental to the execution of a project which is beyond individual capacity. Resources which would otherwise have remained idle have been brought into use by cooperative means.

In ancient and medieval times cooperation developed spontaneously as a sort of mutual aid around irrigation-arrangement, appointment of a common herdsman for a number of farm-families, pooling of milk from all the cows belonging to all the households of a village for making cheese in bulk, workers' guilds for the protection of their interests, etc.

Modern Cooperation

Modern cooperation differs from the ancient form both in spirit and organization. The idea of modern cooperation arose in the wake of acute strife of competitive capitalism which destroyed the concept of mutual aid altogether. "Modern cooperation" as a substitute of competition was the result of search for remedy of the mass poverty and unemployment which followed creation of enormous wealth and its concentration in the hands of a few through the industrial revolution of the 18th and early 19th century.

Robert Owen is considered to be the founder of the modern cooperative movement. He started model factories at New Lanark which were essentially experiments in cooperative production. The essence of the theory of cooperation expounded by him is that the value of a product is mainly due to labour going into it and production should be owned and managed by the cooperative of workers in their own interest.

The early phase of modern cooperative movement was characterized by consumers' cooperatives. One of these cooperatives was Rochdale Society of Equitable Pioneers founded under the influence of King in 1844 at Rochdale — a weavers' town of Great Britain by 28 pioneers most of whom were flannel weavers. The factors which influenced the formation of the Rochdale Society were as follows:

(1) Low wages of the depression.
(2) Crowded and insanitary houses.
(3) Poor quality and high prices of goods sold by retailers.
(4) Oppressive credit trading.

The Projected functions of the society were the following:

(a) Establishment of a store for the sale of foods and clothing,
(b) Building of houses for members,
(c) Organizing workshop for employment of members, and
(d) Founding self-sufficient home colony.

The business operations of the society were,

however, practically concentrated in the following fields:

(a) sale of groceries,
(b) sale of meat, and
(c) Establishment of corn mill.

The Rochdale Society created a body of principles. These are stated below:

(1) Open, voluntary membership.
(2) Fixation of a maximum amount of share that a member could buy.
(3) Democratic control of one-member-one-vote.
(4) Limited interest on capital.
(5) Distribution of dividend among members in proportion to their purchases.
(6) Provision for accumulation of reserves.
(7) Education.
(8) Trade only in pure goods.
(9) True weight and measure.
(10) Religious and Political neutrality.

These rules continued to be fundamental to the organization of a cooperative of any type and are even now followed by cooperatives almost all over the world in the shaping of their structures and functions.

The consumers' cooperation spread to other countries of Europe. It was specially successful in the Scandinavian countries, Sweden, Norway, Denmark and Finland of which Sweden stood foremost in regard to achievement in this field. Its achievements consisted in its ability to meet competition of private monopoly, the high quality of its educative campaigns and the high standard of sale-services offered by the cooperatives.

Consumers' Cooperation in America developed mainly around rural supplies consisting of farm-requisites, household equipments and foodstuffs.

Though cooperation started in the field of consumer stores, in the course of time it spread to other spheres of economic activities including educational campaigns for the promotion of cooperative outlook and efficiency in management.

In the course of historical development competitive capitalism gave way to monopoly capitalism which followed a principle of maximizing profit on the basis of restriction of output and underutilization of productive resources. Modern cooperation in the later phase sought to thrive on the principle of maximizing social benefit by fuller utilization of productive resources rather than labour theory of value.

Cooperative Credit

In the middle of the 19th century economic condition of the peasants of Germany was deplorable. This was aggravated and perpetuated owing to their severe exploitation by the merchant-usurers. Raiffeisen tried to emancipate them from their semi-serfdom condition by organizing them into cooperatives as a measure of self-reliance. The farmer derived the following types of benefits from the cooperative credit banks:

(1) Obtaining capital at a low rate of interest.
(2) Selling his crops to anybody he liked at reasonable prices.
(3) Improvement of the standard of farming through mutual supervision and better supplies.

An important development in farm-cooperative-movement was brought about in the U.S.A. during early 1930s by the legislation creating Farm Credit Administration which in turn founded a system of banks for cooperatives to make facility, operating and commodity loans. The component banks of the Farm Credit Administration are district federal land banks, intermediate credit banks and banks for cooperatives. Share-capital of these banks was initially contributed by the Federal Government. These component banks of the Farm Credit Administration lend funds directly to the farmers' cooperatives known as land banks and production credit associations. By the early 1960s the ownership of capital stock of the lending institutions passed from the Federal Government into the hands of the co-operatives of farmers. The Federal Government also helped in the production of growth of rural electric cooperatives which borrowed funds from the Rural Electrification Administration. In 1955 more than two and a half million farms in addition to many non-farm households, schools, churches and industries of rural areas were receiving service from the rural electricity cooperatives.

Cooperation in Farming

Typical illustrations of bringing idle resources into active uses are furnished by cooperative farming practices in a number of countries. In Italy labour brigades formed cooperatives as a means to large-scale reclamation of land. The first such cooperative farm was organized in Italy in 1886. By 1949 some 150,000 acres came to be farmed in this way. About 70 per cent of the cooperatives were, however, divided into small farms for separate farming. Many of the undivided farms emerged in the process of draining of the Po valley by labour-societies and reclaimed lands ultimately passed into their hands for collective farming.

In Israel cooperative farming originated in the same way as in Italy as a device for reclamation and settlement of new lands. But unlike most of the Italian cooperative farms the cooperative farms of Israel were based on collective farming and living in village communes. The growth of such cooperative village known as kibbutzim was favoured by the peculiar technical and economic conditions of Jewish settlement in Israel and also by the needs of their security among a local population of strangers. According to a study the gross product of the cooperative farms in Israel increased from 1936 to 1960 at as high an annual rate as 11.5 per cent. Two per cent of the annual rate of growth of the gross product was attributed to capital, 1.5 per cent to land and labour, 5 per cent to extended utilization of raw materials and a residual of 3 per cent to technical progress a substantial portion of which was due to capital formation.

In Russia collective farms not only pooling land of the farms but controlling every aspect of their life under centralized planning became the basis of balanced development of agriculture and industry of the country. In fact collective ownership and management of lands became instrumental to transference of a large proportion of rural labour force to the cause of industrial development.

Under the plan of agrarian reforms in Chile fresh settlements were being made with cooperatives of farmers in replacement of landlord estates. Thus, here cooperative farms were instituted as device for transforming big landlord estates into progressive owner operated farms without breaking them up into tiny uneconomic holdings. Elaborate plans of crop-production were drawn up at general conferences of all the members in their planning session.

Cooperation in Economic Crisis

During 1870-76 the Danish farm economy was in the grip of severe crisis. The crisis was precipitated by excessive world supply of grain specially due to the supply from the prairies of the Western States of America competing with Danish grain in the grain-importing industrial countries like Britain. The crisis of the falling price of grain was aggravated by the shortage of gold so much so that Denmark started having imports of grain greater than its exports. The country then set out to exploit the situation by developing dairy production on a cooperative basis which enabled it to tide over the crisis by production at a higher level of efficiency facilitated by the invention of cream-operator and the mechanical churn.

Establishment of cooperative dairies progressed at a great speed in Denmark during the end of the 19th century. The number increased from 176 in 1886 to over 200 in 1888. It reached 942 by 1900. The cream separator and other machinery introduced by cooperative means made possible the savings of a considerable amount of sweated female labour and production of better-quality-products; "They drew the farmers into a new well-organized fellowship of interests quite different in character from the village community a century earlier". The cooperative dairies emerged from "deliberations by practical farmers of how agricultural production and marketing could best be improved". "Through the cooperative dairies many thousands of farmers had become accustomed to the shareholder's delivery undertakings and the needs to subscribe guarantee capital toward erection and management under joint responsibility". "The cooperatives in Denmark strengthened the movement toward independence by making farming profitable even during a severe crisis and by liberating the farmers from dependence on individuals who were invariably their political opponents". The Cooperative Movement in Denmark achieved excellent results by enabling farmers to make use of the scientific experiments of the Royal Veterinary and Agricultural College as well as technical and general educational work of the agricultural societies and schools. The Danish case furnishes an excellent example of how cooperation could help an economy tide over a crisis.

Cooperative Supply

Cooperation for the supply of farm requisites was motivated by the farmers' desire to get their requirements in good quality and at moderate prices. In fact this was a measure against the fraudulent methods followed by the private traders in selling goods required for farm production.

The Agricultural and Horticultural Association founded in 1867 in London, the Irish Agricultural Organization Society founded in 1894 under the leadership of Horace Plunket and the establishment of a similar organization in England and Scotland during 1900-5 gave great impetus to the promotion of agricultural cooperatives for supply of farm requisites. Agricultural Cooperation in Great Britain is mainly preoccupied with supply though structurally it consists mostly of multipurpose societies. In 1950s such societies had a turnover of £ 80,000,000 mostly comprising food stuffs, fertilizers, seeds, implements and other farm requisites.

Many cooperatives in England were preoccupied with selling petroleum products to farmers. They had their own tank vehicles for the purpose.

In the United States there are many large regional wholesale societies. They supply to the farmers farm requisites through their branch stores and affiliated local association. The goods sold are mostly feeding stuff, petroleum products and fertilizers. In the United States there was a tendency on the part of the consumer cooperatives to enter also the field of supply of farm requisites.

In Germany cooperation in the supply of agricultural requirements developed as consequence of the cooperative credit banks taking over supply activities. Orders for supplies collected from members are placed in bulk with a regional supply federation which, in turn, also buys farmers' grain. In France the local agent of a regional supply association is the syndicate Agricole.

In Denmark each commodity has its specialized supply organization. Cooperatives for supply of farm requisites have served in recent years as the agencies for technological innovation in farming by bringing the new inventions of science in the form of new inputs within the reach of the farmers. In this way these bodies have contributed towards raising the standard of farming.

Marketing Cooperatives

Marketing cooperatives developed from the need of sending products to distant places for higher prices and returns that could not be arranged by producers individually. Cooperatives could make goods more valuable by better marketing arrangements which could not be done by individuals. Marketing cooperatives developed more in the United States than in other countries because in the United States distances from the production areas to market areas were greatest and also the production areas were too scattered to permit local processing.

Cooperative marketing of wheat in Canada with its basis in three pools one each for Alberta, Saakatchewan and Manitoba was on the whole very much successful in spite of the reverses it faced during the Great Depression of the thirties.

Cooperative marketing has excellent scope in respect of fruit and vegetables which are highly perishable. The Cooperative Citras Exchange of California and Florida furnished striking example of success in the handling of orange, lemons and grapefruits.

In the Netherlands and England perishable fruit, vegetables and flowers were successfully handled by the cooperative auction market.

Cooperative Services

Cooperative was not confined to the fields of buying, selling, production, processing and credit. Cooperation also developed to a large extent for the provision of services of different types. Thus, health societies were organized in some parts of India for the eradication of Malaria. The societies maintained doctors and distributed medicines among members. Contributions of members were used to meet their expenses. Eradication of Malaria contributed to improvement of the efficiency of labour in agricultural production.

Cooperatives also played a very important role in the supply of electricity, and sometimes by means of their own generators. The Cooperatives for supply of electricity developed in large number in Czechoslovakia, Germany, France, Northern Sweden and U.S.A.

An electricity cooperative was formed by persons of a locality willing to buy electricity who contributed capital towards cost of supply-arrangement (e.g., construction of lines and transformers) made by a public utility company. Such a public utility company in its turn might be formed by a number of village cooperatives in collaboration with the municipal authorities of the neighbouring town.

The pressure of need for farm-mechanization to increase food-production during the Second World War and the period following it encouraged formation of machinery using cooperatives to make such use economic.

In addition to above, there also developed some other types of service cooperatives, e.g., cooperative transport societies running buses, taxies, ferries, etc., cooperative cold storage locker, community canning centres preserving fruits and vegetables, cooperative housing societies helping poor people acquire houses.

In some Balkan countries cooperative housing societies were instrumental in the pooling of voluntary labour and making of building materials for the purpose of replacement of ill-equipped old houses by scientifically planned new houses. This device was followed for remodelling a village from one end to the other.

Some Recent Trends and Concepts

The speciality of recent trends and concepts in agricultural cooperation consists in an integrated approach to the problem of agricultural development which is designed to release a momentum for sustained development. This implies an effective coordination of credit, farm supplies, production, marketing, net savings and capital formation. In older days the cooperative movement attached excessive importance to its credit aspect. Experience of the past in India and other countries has shown that when the cooperative movement was centered on credit alone it was destined to failure because of non-repayment of debts followed by the emergence of huge overdue loans. When the movement is confined to granting loans without any responsibility of insuring their proper utilization it does not promote self-reliance by enabling the borrowers to free themselves from the causes of their poverty and indebtedness. This view evolved into the idea of supervised credit based on integration of credit and extension services.

The integration of credit programmes with extension services directed towards tangible improvement of agriculture has already been instituted in a number of countries like Brazil, Mexico and India. The extension services in these countries have gone a longway towards accelerating the educational process for the development of cooperation.

Supervision begins with the preparation of the farm plan in the formulation of which the extension agents help the farmers. It has also been observed that the linking of credit with a farm plan goes so far as to actually supply the loan in the form of inputs required by the plan.

Mere improvement of production often becomes ineffective unless it is supported by marketing outlets. In recent years, therefore, cooperatives have tended to combine marketing with production of processing activities. In fact, organized marketing has opened up new possibilities of production. The revitalized FaCoMas (Farm Cooperative Marketing Associations) of the Philippines offer good examples of co-ordination between production and marketing.

Recent times have witnessed development of cooperatives as agency of economic development. An excellent example of this process is furnished by the Cooperative Dairy union of the Kaira district of Gujarat in India which was established on April 1, 1946. It originated from the scheme of the Government of Bombay to supply milk at reasonable prices for expectant mothers and children. Though the scheme started with buying milk from a private dairy, it was eventually replaced by the cooperative mentioned above to ensure larger share for the producers in the prices paid by the consumers. On March 31, 1965 the total assets of the society were $ 7,586,000. The paid up share capital was $ 264,000. In 1964-65 the retained profits from the business amounted to $ 1,298,000. The activities of the cooperative were, however, not confined to the collection, processing of milk and the marketing of the dairy products. It extended its activities to the promotion of an improved breeding centre, a veterinary programme and a feed-improvement programme. In addition, the union rendered technical help to the village cooperatives to improve land and village roads and vastly contributed to extension services for changing the traditional habits of the rural people and promotion of application of modern science. Thus the union served as an engine for social and economic development of the surrounding rural area.

The success of the Japanese cooperatives is mainly due to the organization of a network of cooperatives in the villages bringing every farm within the scope of cooperative services. These cooperatives combine marketing, purchasing and production and thus maximize economic services to the farmer.

The test of a cooperative movement consists in how far it has been able to release the forces of development by increasing capital and by introducing technical innovation through the elevation of the attitudes of the people.

The new concept of cooperative credit is to multiply itself through new savings in conjunction with a state-sponsored programme of technological innovations pursued by the National Extension Services. This would be creative and dynamic credit. Even a relaxation of usual restrictions on lending in respect of security, amount and formalities can strengthen this type of credit resting on effective technical and administrative supervision. Relaxation of restrictions would have its basis in productiveness of the credit.

Theory of Cooperative in the Context of Development

From the above survey it seems obvious that there are a number of ways in which cooperatives have opened up or can open up possibilities of further development of agricultural economy.

First, they help in counteracting restriction on supply imposed by monopolistic combinations in business. Efficient functioning of the capitalist economy is possible when perfect competition among different firms is assured. The principle of efficiency would drive each firm to minimum cost and maximum output position. And price in the long run is no more than what is equal to the minimum cost per unit of output. If the price is higher than the minimum cost, supply would increase by entry of new farms to the business until the price under the pressure of additional supply comes down to the minimum cost. If the price is lower than the minimum cost supply would be cut down by exit of some firms of the business or by reduction of supplies of the existing firms until the price rises to be equal to cost. This is an idealistic condition of perfect competition which does not tend to prevail in reality for long. Under the condition of diminishing cost many firms which are unable to take advantage of the economies of scale are forced to drop out in the process of cut-throat competition. Other firms remaining in the field enter into monopolistic combination under which equilibrium output indicated by the point of equality between marginal revenue and marginal cost (the output giving maximum profit) is obtained below the level of optimum output obtained under perfect competition. In these circumstances smaller firms by forming cooperatives contribute to maintaining competition and continuing the operation of the forces of expansion of output.

In developing economies big estates or large holdings are often found to be responsible for under-utilization of the land-resources. Large holdings which cannot all be managed under owner cultivation tend to be leased out to share-croppers who would lack adequate capital for fullest possible use of the leased lands. Big estates broken up into smaller pieces and then placed under cooperative management of larger number of small owner farms would pave the way to fuller utilization of the lands. Cooperatives, again, would stimulate development by democratizing credit. Smaller farms having idle labour-capacity or land-resource or any type of idle fixed-capital resource have been enabled by cooperative credit to make its proper use in contributing to expansion of output.

Cooperatives, also, as public organizations have contributed to the supply of business knowledge. It is well-known that private business concerns are reluctant to disseminate business knowledge. This is because it invites competition. An individual of small means is reluctant to run the risk of acquiring knowledge through experience of doing the business. A cooperative by pooling this risk helps substantially in the accumulation of business experience which, again, is easily communicable to people at large because of its public character.

Postscript

Israel

Different types of cooperative farming developed in Israel. The difference from each other consisted in difference of the type of relationship between the individual household and the cooperative.

Kibbutz is characterized by common ownership of the means of production and collective management of the economic and non-economic activities undertaken.

Activities of Kibbutz are comprehensive, covering production, consumer services, education and cultural programmes.

Moshav is a type of cooperative village where cultivation is done by individual families, but supplies and marketing are in the hands of cooperatives. Facilities for storage and marketing are located at regional centres and run by the cooperative society.

Moshavshitufi is a collective village where productive resources are collectively owned and operated for common benefit of the villagers. People, however, in such a village live in their own respective families.

Recent years, however, have witnessed shift of emphasis from Kibbutz to Moshav where the role of the individual family is more pronounced than that of the cooperative.

The policy of rural development in Israel is for cooperatives to promote integration of agricultural and industrial activities.

China

Attempt was made to promote the rural economy of China through cooperatives following land-reforms between 1950-52, redistributing lands to the landless and tenant farmers. This process developed into large-scale public ownership of land and other means of production around 1958. It was accompanied by Advanced Agricultural Producer's Cooperative (AAPC), involving large units of management and village communes. However, extreme egalitarian principle in income distribution and concentration of management brought the cooperative rural economy of China to the verge of collapse during mid-1970s.

The year 1978 was marked by a sharp change in the rural cooperative economy in China. The change consisted in the introduction of household management into the cooperative system and joint ventures of various management forms. There, also, developed a great emphasis on rural industrial cooperatives which by 1985 figured high in the rural economy. Moreover, collective type farm cooperatives gave way to service cooperatives, such as marketing, supplies and credit in which voluntary spirit is very strong. Also, cooperatives were used as a means to rural capital formation.

REFERENCES

Digby, Margaret, *The World Cooperative Movement*, Hutchinson University, London.

Smith, Louis P.F., *The Evolution of Agricultural Cooperation*, Basil Blackwell, Oxford, 1961, chs 1, 2, 4.

Skrubbeltrang, F., Agricultural Development and Rural Reform in Denmark, FAO, Rome 1953, p. 189, p.199, p.202, p.219.

New Approach to Agricultural Credit, FAO Agricultural Development Paper No. 77, Rome, 1964.

Farmer Cooperative in the United States, US Department of Agriculture, Washington, 1955.

International Cooperative Training Journal, Madison, Wisconsin, USA, Vol 3, No. 4.

A Study into the structure and Functioning of the Farmers' Cooperative Marketing Associations in the Province of Cotabato, MIT-UNESCO Project (mimeo), 1968 and in the Province of Nueva Ecija, Central Luzan State University-UNESCO Project (mimeo), Philippines, 1969.

Ogura, Takekaza, Agricultural Development in Modern Japan, Japan — FAO, Association, 1963 pp. 668-675.

Ulrey, Orion, The Cooperative: An Agency for Rural Development (The Kaira District Cooperative Milk Producer's Union Ltd, Anand, Gujarat State, India), Department of Agricultural Economics, Michigan State University, March 1966.

Sadan, Ezra, "Capital Formation and Growth in the Israel Cooperative Farm", *American Journal of Agricultural Economics*, Vol 50, November 1968.

A Study into the working of Pilot Project Farming Societies in East India, Agro-Economic Research Centre, Visva-Bharati, 1966.

Mandal, G.C., "Agricultural Cooperatives in Japan", *Economic and Political Weekly*, Bombay, Vol V, No 39, Review of Agriculture, September 26, 1970.

Weitz, Raanan, "Rural Development : The Lessons of Israel and Implications for China" in *China's Rural Development, Miracle*, John W. Longworth (ed.), IAAE Queensland, 1987.

Simei, Wen, "Development of the Cooperative Economy in Rural China", 1987, *Ibid.*

10

TOWARD A CULTURAL REVOLUTION

A

THE BREAKDOWN of community relations in India is rather premature. It is premature in the sense that market as a possible substitute of community relations is still unable to cope with the task of rural development. Had market forces been developed and free from distortion, rural resources would have been brought into greater use, giving greater material welfare to the villagers, particularly landless agricultural labourers who constitute a substantial part of the rural community.

Imperfections of markets account for to a large extent the urban-rural differential in per worker income. Per worker urban income is five times higher than the per worker rural income.[1] This is a symptom of technological imbalance between the rural and the urban sector. This implies that the process of diffusion of higher technology and capital-investment is hampered by monopolistic tendencies. Thus the pace of urbanization is slackened. On the one hand there is enormous concentration of wealth in big cities, on the other hand stagnation persists in small towns.

B

Urban areas are superior to rural areas in almost all

respects. Thus, per capita urban income in much higher than per capita rural income, the rate of literacy is much higher in urban areas than in rural areas, rate of infant mortality is much higher in rural areas than in urban areas, technology is much superior in urban areas to that in rural areas. Therefore, the objective of rural development is to minimize urban-rural differential. Most essential step toward this is to remove the infrastructural deficiency of the rural sector in respect of power, transportation, irrigation, health services and technical education.

C

Potentiality of land reforms as a factor in rural development is limited in view of the extreme scarcity of land-resource in comparison with the size of population depending on it. Unless alternative assets like technical skill, water and industrial estates are brought into usable form, rural development is bound to be halted.

Higher agricultural technology if widespread would lead to fuller utilization of the existing land-resource. The current higher technologies in agriculture are not adapted to various environmental conditions. Thus, high-yielding varieties of rice are not effective for the *Kharif* season. The cloudy skies of the *Kharif* season are not favourable to photo-synthesis which is essential for high yield.[2] India's need to develop a variety of rice suitable even for the *Kharif* season is still unfulfilled. Since this is the major season of rice crop overall rice yield is still not satisfactory. Progress is still awaited in respect of drought-tolerant and flood resistant varieties. This is because drought and flood-prone areas are vast in the country. Agricultural development and, for that matter, rural development would warrant in India tremendous experiments with environment which is characterized by bewildering variety in respect of climatic conditions, topography, social and water-resource. India is in need of an appropriate technology in rural areas which is well-suited to ecological balance. As the resources are scarce, their productivity can be optimized only by scientific adaptation of technology and management.

D

It is obvious that there should be more technical content in rural education. Since durable consumer goods and household equipments like transistors, television, bicycles, furniture etc. are spreading more and more even in rural areas repair services required by these articles will be in greater demand. Suitable training for turning out skilled labour for these purposes would meet a real need for rural employment. Carpentry, masonry, electrical fittings, tube-wells, and pumpsets repairing etc. should demand skilled labour more and more with expansion of construction and farm business. The system of rural education should make provision for the promotion of such labour.

In fact, adequate importance has not been attached to rural education as an agency of change in various aspects of life, e.g., social structure, style of living, cultural outlook, technology and economy. Contribution of education or rather interaction between education and economic development have been undermined. A study indicates that rank correlation between per capita income and rate of adult literacy (per cent) in 12 South, South-east and Far East Asian countries is highly significant (+0.71).[3] Thus the relationship between the economic level and literacy can be neglected with great detriment to the national economy.

Since literacy is the highest medium of education, it is highly significant as a creative force. But sluggishness of demand for literacy and education is widespread among scheduled caste, scheduled tribe and other backward communities. This is not simply due to poverty. But retrogressive caste tradition is itself a drag on progress of literacy and education.[4] In this way it reacts adversely on economic growth and tends to perpetuate poverty.

It has been observed that though schooling facilities are a very important factor in education their inadequacy is not a stumbling block in the way of universalization of literacy. Of foremost importance is the creation of a socio-cultural climate favourable to generating an appropriate motivation of the people. The socio-institutional environment should be moulded and directed to overcome the deficiency in demand of people for literacy and education. Services of voluntary associations may be utilized by concerned Government departments in the task. Conferences of school teachers and educationists may be held under their auspices from time-to-time with a view to promoting this objective.[5]

As has been observed earlier, poverty may be responsible for the deficiency in demand for education to some extent but not directly. This is because primary education is costless at present and a few children below 12 are nowadays found to be engaged in money earning activities. The real obstacle to school-going seems to be the stagnant economic condition which thwarts all hopes of change for the better through education and the consequent lack of appreciation of the utility of education.[6]

The fact that urban rate of literacy is much higher than the rural rate is explained by the more progressive character of the urban society in economic, social and cultural respects. What is, therefore, necessary is to set in motion the process of modernization in economy that will release forces to weaken the bond of tradition. In this perspective a technological revolution is the crying need of the hour. It results not only in economic revolution it attains its culmination in a cultural revolution which liberates man from slavery of manual labour and upholds his dignity. It kindles the aspiration of man for a better life. It substitutes science for superstition, reason for tradition. It liberates outlook both of the "superior" and the "inferior" forging social homogeneity. Above all, introduction of labour-saving technology into production is the best way of defeating contempt for manual labour, awakening the toilers to their rightful place in the sun. Facilities of education would go on beaing unutilized or under-utilized until the basic transformation of technology, society and culture is brought about.

Colleges of education could be expected, as a part of experimental research in education, to evolve models which would combine economic activities with more scientific techniques and literary education for popularizing book-education. Empirical findings, suggest that a poor tradition-bound rural society needs something like this which results in a cultural revolution wiping out the retrogressive forces of tradition and degradation. Periodical conferences of primary school teachers under the auspices of voluntary associations mentioned before could perhaps arouse their conscience and responsibility as potential agents of technological, social and cultural changes.

E

An appropriate post-graduate programme for rural area is also a crucial question worthy of special consideration. Of foremost relevance to the task is the pattern of growth in the rural economy. If the major component of growth is production, the major agents of growth in our rural economy are the farmers. It is they who can profit by the growth of production in their own interest. Some non-agricultural enterprises also need to grow as a part of the development process to reduce the excessive dependence on agriculture.

If a future economy is composed of 60 per cent workers engaged in agriculture, and 40 per cent in industries and services instead of 70 per cent and 30 per cent, respectively, as at present, the system of training and education must adapt and change. In fact, it must address itself to the promotion of a new economy and the economic logic of the projected change.

The social goals such as the level of literacy and school education which would generate the outlook, values and urge for a better life are no less important than the economic ones. These were expected by the Indian Education Commission (1966) to result in a "social and cultural revolution".

The educational goals documented by the Commission were: "to bring about major improvement in the effectiveness of primary education; to introduce work experience as an integral element of general education; to vocationalize secondary education; to improve the quality of teachers at all levels and to provide teachers in sufficient strength to liquidate illiteracy; to strengthen centres of advanced study and strive to attain in some of our universities at least higher international standards; to lay special emphasis on the combination of teaching and research in agriculture and allied sciences".

As regards school education Gunnar Myrdal, the renowned economist, was convinced that this task could not be fulfilled "without teachers who are not only satisfied with their economic and social conditions and are accepted as intellectual and moral leaders in their community, but who are also enthusiastic and imbued with the zeal to disseminate useful and practical knowledge and with the will to advance".[7]

Professor Myrdal, therefore, considered the institutions for teacher training as strategically important in educational reform. "They should be considered as Power Plants that generate moral and intellectual energy among the students to prepare the people for development".[8]

These thoughts should well provide a framework of an appropriate programme for education and training for development. One part of the programme needs to be developed to training teachers for the primary and secondary level and another part will have to be directed toward creating technical personnel.

The centres for rural studies which are poised for the adoption of educational programme will have to encounter the problem of a liberal bias since the scholars themselves are from this tradition. The mere addition of the term 'rural' to all social science subjects, – rural economics, rural sociology, rural finance etc. will hardly suffice. However, liberal education need not be discarded altogether, perhaps the centres would need to frame a composite course, covering the science and technology involved in actual production as well as social sciences relevant to the task of management and institution-building.

It should lead to striking a balance between the liberal social sciences and the technology of production.

A vital aspect of the programme is the special character of teaching methods which is likely to distinguish it from the usual teaching of social sciences. The training programme for rural development can assume great significance if it uses research as its tool and if it integrates research with training. The point is that every idea should be subject to empirical verification. Every topic has its laboratory counterpart out in the field.

The question may arise about the market for a programme like this. The gap between desirability and effective demand is as old as human society. It is well-known that social welfare can be improved by placing more money in the hands of the poor. But the market mechanism does not work accordingly. It is distorted by unequal distribution of resources and facilities. The established pattern of market mechanism is not favourable to rural development, because most of the efficient technology and means of production are at the disposal of the urban sector and most of the poor are located in the rural sector. The market is not in a position to direct the flow of funds and knowledge into the rural sector.

However, in a democratic society the need of the majority are bound to enter into national planning and influence the determination of social priorities. The institution of rural services is inherent in this process: A classic example is Rabindranath Tagore's Department of Rural Reconstruction. Once extensive rural services are established the courses to be offered by the centres of rural studies can be enlivened by an appropriate motivation and a sense of urgency and direction. Only this can prevent any programme from sinking into the stupor of an ineffectual literary culture and prevent students from becoming "deskmen, not spoiling their hands".[9]

The introduction of rural services and the conversion of teaching into a learning process can infuse a new spirit into rural education which is indispensable for development.

F

High demographic pressure is a stagnating or retrogressive factor in the rural economy and society. The role of family planning, is, therefore, enormous. Family planning becomes complex in the face of high rates of infant mortality. So long as the rate of survival of infants is low, females in the child-bearing age would like to have more children. In this context contraceptive measures are likely to meet resistance.

Cultural revolution has to make significant contribution to family planning by elevating the degree of awareness of child-care-measures and the contribution of children, negative or positive, to family welfare.

While the new-born must be given utmost care so that healthy development of a few children dispenses with the need of additional children, negative contribution of many children needs to be properly appreciated. Stephen Enke writes:[10] "High fertility rates have the demographic effect of increasing the proportionate number of children. A country with a crude birth rate of over 40/1000 a year is likely to have over 40 per cent of its population under 15 years of age. Youngsters under 15 years of age are significant consumers but insignificant producers. Large families including many children with consequently low incomes per family member are poor contributors to domestic saving. Low savings per capita are associated with young populations and high fertility".

It is conceivable that a dependence – load of 2/5th of the family members is a drag on progress of economic welfare. It is likely to pull down the economy to a level of bare subsistence. This is why the importance of population is not less than that of growth of output.

Lower birth rate per 1000 is indeed a sign of socio-cultural progress and a step toward economic progress, too. Higher rate of literacy in Kerala (69 per cent of 1981-Census) as compared with that in West Bengal (41%) and all-India (37%) was largely due to influences of Christian Missionaries.[11] In addition to the contribution of better health services of Kerala in comparison with those of West Bengal, it is higher level of literacy in Kerala that might be supposed to have played an important part in lowering the crude birth per 1000 from 31.9 of 1970 to 25.3 of 1978, while the corresponding rate in West Bengal increased from 29.9 of 1970 to 30.4 of 1978.[12]

Change in technology is not the only object of cultural revolution. One of its other objects no less in importance should be to generate a concept of rational family planning. Size of population in India compared to resources is so vast that even zero growth might be covetable for its economic progress. Overcrowded villages are as much responsible for environmental pollution in rural areas in the form of poor sanitation and lavatory facilities and scarcity of pure drinking water as big industries for urban areas. A cleaner rural area free from pollution should be as much an object of family planning as higher per capita income.

Cultural revolution is expected to produce a society not only free from exploitation but free from ignorance, superstition, squalor, malnutrition and poor vitality. Community-relations, community consciousness and community actions need to be called forth to fight against all these conditions of cultural degradation.

NOTES

1. Gobinda C. Mandal, *Technology, Growth and Welfare in Indian Agriculture*, Agricole Publishing Academy, New Delhi, 1989, Chapter 7.
2. G.C. Mandal, Technology, Growth and Welfare in Indian Agriculture: A Case Study in West Bengal, Agro-Economic Research Centre, Visva-Bharati, Santiniketan, 1987, mimeo. p.2.
3. Gobinda C. Mandal, The Problem of Literacy and Education Among Scheduled Caste Girls — A Social Analysis, 1989, Chapter 2 (The Role of Education in Social and Economic Development) (unpublished).
4. *Ibid.*
5. *Ibid.*
6. *Ibid.*
7. Gunnar Myrdal, *The Challenge of World Poverty*, Penguin Books, 1976, p.205.
8. Gunnar Myrdal, *Ibid.*
9. Gunnar Myrdal, *Ibid.*
10. Stephen Enke, "Economic Consequences of Rapid Population Growth", *Economic Journal*, London, December 1971.
11. Moni Nag "Fertility Differential in Kerala and West Bengal", *Economic and Political Weekly*, Vol. XIX, No. 1, January 7, 1984
12. Moni Nag, *Ibid.*

APPENDICES

APPENDIX-A

The Nature of India's Self-sufficiency in Foodgrains

Production of Foodgrains (Thousand tonnes)

Year	Total Cereals	Total foodgrains
1950-51	42,414	50,895
1960-61	69,314	82,018
1970-71	96,604	108,422
1980-81	118,962	129,589
1983-84	139,481	152,374
1984-85	133,579	145,539
1985-86	137,079	150,440
1986-87	132,331	144,069
1987-88	129,390	140,350
1988-89	156,550	170,250

There was substantial increase in production of cereals and total foodgrains during 1950-87. While production of cereals stood at 157 million tonnes, production of total foodgrains attained the high figure of 170 million tonnes in 1988-89. It was possible to reduce total import of foodgrains (rice and wheat) to about 1.1 million tonnes by 1984-85. In 1985-86 only 10,000 tonnes of foodgrains were imported. By 1986-87 the import of foodgrains was absolutely dispensed with and export of wheat rose from one lakh to 3.39 lakh tonnes by 1985-86. This was a laudable achievement in terms of national self-sufficiency. However, still there is a long way to go toward defeating the widespread malnutrition among the masses of people.[1] (*cf.* Chapter 2)

1. Directorate of Economics and Statistics, Department of Agriculture and Cooperation, Ministry of Agriculture, Government of India, Indian Agriculture, in Brief, 22nd edition, New Delhi, 1988, pp.44 and 64. Also, Government of India, Economic Survey 1989-90.

APPENDIX-B

Some Statistics Relating to Indian Foreign Trade[1]

(Rs. in crores)

Year	Exports: Exports of agricultural commodities from India	Exports: Total exports from India	Exports: % share of agricultural exports	Imports: Imports of selected agricultural commodities	Imports: Total imports into India	Imports: % share of agricultural imports
1965-66	334.9	805.6	41.6	535.7	1394.1	30.4
1975-76	1685.5	4042.3	41.9	2142.0	5265.2	40.7
1985-86	3271.5	10874.6	30.0	3884.8	19665.4	19.8

Trade Balance of India (Rs. in crores)

Year	Amount
1965-66	– 588.5
1975-76	– 1222.9
1985-86	– 8790.8
1987-88	– 9296.1

In 1965-66 India's trade deficit was to the tune of Rs. 588.5 crores which increased to Rs. 1222.9 crores in 1975-76. The deficit widened to Rs. 9296.1 crores by 1987-88. Percentage of agricultural commodities in both exports and imports declined. (*cf.* Chapter 3)

1. Directorate of Economics and Statistics, Department of Agriculture and Cooperation, Ministry of Agriculture, Government of India, Indian Agriculture in Brief, New Delhi, 1988, p. 101. Also, Government of India, Economic Survey 1989-90.

APPENDIX-C

Some Statistics Relating to Cooperatives in Indian Agriculture and Rural Economy[1]

Item	1960-61	1984-85
A. Primary Agricultural Societies		
(a) No. in lakhs	2.12	0.92
(b) Percentage of villages covered	75	97
(c) Paid up share capital (Rs. crores)	57.75	778.66
(d) Working capital (Rs. crores)	273.92	5911.22
(e) Loans advanced (Rs. crores)	202.75	2693.01
B. Land Development Banks (for long term loans)		
(a) Central (No.)	18	19
(b) Primary (No.)	463	890
(c) Loans Advanced to individuals (Rs. crores)	11.62	453.37
C. Cooperative Milk Supply Unions		
(a) No.	94	225
(b) Paid up share capital (Rs. crores)	0.20	30.48
(c) Value of Sales (Rs. crores)	4.72	809.86

1. Directorate of Economics and Statistics, Department of Agriculture and Cooperation, Ministry of Agriculture, Government of India, Indian Agriculture in Brief, New Delhi, 1988, pp. 88-90, 91, 95-96.

D. Fishery Cooperatives		
(a) No. of societies	2355	7542.46
(b) Value of sales (Rs. crores)	1.07	20.54
E. Total Institutional credit for Agriculture (including credit supplied by Regional Rural Banks and Commercial Banks) (Rs. crores)	214.35	9644.46

Statistics relating to agricultural cooperatives and rural credit indicate vast expansion. Net National Agricultural Product amounted to Rs. 57331 crores in 1984-85. We may roughly estimate that agricultural credit is 9644/57331 × 100 = 17 per cent of Net National Agricultural Product.

If we suppose that productivity of capital is 30 per cent, then it may be estimated that 5 per cent of the Net National Agricultural Product is due to credit. Thus, there is still vast scope of expansion of agricultural production through credit.

Dairy Cooperative, however, registered about 172 times increase in the volume of business (sales), whereas sales of fishery cooperatives increased 19 times during 1960-85 (*cf.* Chapter 9).

The total value of assets of the Dairy Union of the Kaira District of Gujarat rose from about Rs. 7 crores in 1965 (*cf.* Chapter 9) to about Rs. 24.34 crores. The sales of the Dairy Union amounted to about Rs. 152.50 crores in 1987-88[2]. Thus, taken singly dairy is the field where cooperative enterprise achieved remarkable success.

2. 42nd Annual Report 1987-88 of the Kaira District Cooperative Milk Producers' Union, Anand.

APPENDIX-D

Rural Development Programmes

On the basis of the 32nd Round of National Sample Survey (1977-78) percentage of persons below poverty line was estimated at 51.2 for rural areas and 38.2 for urban areas. However, the 38th Round of the Survey indicated a decline of persons below poverty line by 12.5 per cent in rural areas and 7.8 per cent in urban areas.

The central objective of all rural development programmes of India is to raise people above poverty line. These programmes include National Rural Employment Programme (NREP), Rural Landless Employment Guarantee Programme (RLEGP), Training of Rural Youth for Self Employment (TRYSEM), Drought Prone and other Area Programmes and Integrated Rural Development Programme.

National Rural Employment Programme (NREP)

The Food For Work Programme was restricted and renewed as NREP from October 1980. This is being implemented by States as a centrally sponsored programme with 50 per cent central assistance. The scheme aims at creating additional employment opportunities for unemployed and underemployed persons in rural areas which are expected to result in the formation of productive community assets for strengthening rural economic and social infrastructure and improving the overall quality of life. The onset of drought conditions induced projects like irrigation works, rural water supply works, renovation of village tank etc. In the Seventh Plan Period an outlay of Rs. 2487 crores was allotted to NREP, generating 1476 million mandays of employment during the first four years of Plan.

Rural Landless Employment Guarantee Programme (RLEGP)

It was started in some States as 100 per cent centrally supported scheme to offer employment to at lest one member of every family of every rural landless labourer for a minimum period of 100 days in a year. Indira Awas Yojana, a part of the RLEGP has been launched to provide housing facilities to shelterless persons. This scheme provides for the distribution of surplus lands above ceiling among landless labourers for the improvement of their standard of living.

In 1989-90 a new employment programme designated as Jawahar Rozgar Yojana was launched. In fact, NREP and RLEGP and the Jawahar Rozgar Yojana have been integrated into the new programmes to generate 837 million mandays of employment at a cost of Rs. 2623 crores through rural works, creating durable community assets specially for poverty alleviation.

Training of Rural Youth for Self Employment (TRYSEM)

The main thrust of this scheme is on equipping rural youth (18-35 years of age) with necessary skills and technical knowledge to take up vocations of self-employment in the field of agriculture and allied activities. However, up to this day the scheme did not appear to have aroused mass enthusiasm to any significant extent. This may be due to lack of other supporting facilities, e.g. supply of finance, working space, marketing etc.

Drought Prone Area Programme (DPAP)

Drought Prone Area Programme was initiated in 1970 with a view to developing areas and improving the socio-economic conditions of their inhabitants by providing them with employment opportunities.

Integrated Rural Development (IRDP)

Integrated Rural Development Programme (IRDP) which came into existence in 1976 incorporated a group of programmes like Drought Prone Area Programme (DPAP), Small Farmers' Development Agency (SFDA), Command Area Development Programme, Development of Desert Area Programmes etc.

IRDP attempts to enlist families with income below Rs. 4800 per annum with a view to making available to them subsidized credit meant for the creation of income generating assets.

Total number of beneficiaries covered by the Integrated Rural Development Programme all over India was 30.27 lakh and the total amount of investment under the programme was Rs. 1329.69 lakhs in 1984-85. Total employment generated under the National Employment Programme amounted to 3953.92 lakh man-days in 1986-87.*

---

* Source of Information :

(a) Government of Orissa, Economic Survey, 1988-89.
(b) Directorate of Economics and Statistics, Department of Agriculture and Cooperation, Ministry of Agriculture, Government of India, Indian Agricultural in Brief, 22nd Edition, New Delhi 1988.
(c) Government of India, Economic Survey, 1989-90.

APPENDIX E

A Review of Recent Literature on Land Reforms

A considerable amount of literature has grown around the comparative merits of 'owner farming', 'share-cropping tenancy', and 'fixed rent tenancy'.

Traditional literature on land-tenure system has looked upon share-cropping tenancy as an inefficient system which prevents realization of the optimum output by reducing the marginal return to labour which is equated to wage-rate at a lower level of equilibrium (E.O. Heady, Economics of Farm Leasing System, *Journal of Farm Economics*, Vol. 29, 1947).

More recent support of the traditional theory is found to some extent in Pronab Bardhan and T.N. Srinivasan (Crop-sharing Tenancy in Agriculture : A Theoretical and Empirical Analysis, *American Economic Review*, Vol. 61, 1971) and more fully in Clive Bell ("Alternative Theories of Share-cropping. Some Tests using evidence from North-east India; *Journal of Development Studies*, Vol.13, 1977).

Opposition to the traditional theory was aroused by lack of evidence of significant differences in yield-rates between share-tenant and owner-farms. Critics of the traditional theory include R. Albert Berry and Welliam R. Clive (Agrarian Structure and Productivity in Developing Countries, John Hopkins University Press, 1979), Yujiro Hayami (Asian Village Economy at the Cross Road, The John Hopkins University Press, 1982), Samar K. Datta and Jeffrey B Nugent (Tenancy Choice in a Competitive

Framework with Transactions Cost. University of South California, 1982). The main thrust of their argument is exploring the possibility of contractual arrangement that would in a competitive condition, eliminates the difference in efficiency between share-tenancy and owner-farming or leasehold tenancy as well as the difference between the return to labour in share-tenancy and the market wage-rate. In a land scarce and labour abundant economy the optimum position that would minimize transactions cost, maximize profit and return to labour could be arrived at by a suitable allocation of land between share-cropping and owner-cultivation along with suitable stipulations of contract about quantum of labour, wage rate and output sharing (Samar K. Datta and Jeffrey B. Nugent, *op. cit.*).

Also, theories of malnutrition and rural poverty were developing around the question of land-distribution (J.E. Stiglitz, The Efficiency Wage Hypothesis, Surplus Labour and the Distribution of Income in LDC's, Oxford Economic Papers 1981; Partha Dasgupta, "An Economic Theory of Malnutrition", Stanford University and London School of Economics). These have a broad relevance to the problem of finding an appropriate agrarian system.

In the wake of large-scale evictions of share-tenants and resumption of owner-cultivation recent land legislation in West Bengal launched a programme for the recording of names of share-croppers and their rights (known as 'Operation Barga') and introduced certain stipulations about output and cost-sharing as a consequence of which the operation of the lease-market and contractual arrangements in farm management has been restricted. The equity consideration seems to be overriding in such a situation (D. Bandyopadhyay, 'Land Reforms in West Bengal', Government of West Bengal, Calcutta 1980; Biplab Dasgupta, "Share-cropping in West Bengal", *Economic and Political Weekly*, Review of Agriculture, 31 March 1984 and 30 June, 1984); Ajit K. Ghose's criticism of 'Operation Barga' in Ajit Kumar Ghose, "Agrarian Reforms in West Bengal : Objectives, Achievements and Limitations", (I.L.O., World Employment Programme Research, Working Paper, Geneva 1980) focuses on its effect of institutionalization the existing distribution of land and repeasantising the agrarian system. Another critique points to the deterrents which recent land legislation of West Bengal is likely to present to the technological progress of agriculture of the State (G.C. Mandal, "Land Reforms in the Context of Agricultural Development with Special Reference to West Bengal", in Manjula Bose (ed.), Land Reforms in Eastern India, Jadavpur University, Calcutta (1981).

Studies documented by the International Rice Research Institute in the volume "Changes in Rice Farming in Selected Areas of Asia", 1975 include observation that in the Philippines share-tenancy and small farm size have not deterred the adoption of modern varieties than did owner-operations (Gelia T. Castillo, p. 355).

INDEX